Bake, Love, Write:

105 Authors Share

Dessert Recipes

and

Advice on Love and Writing

EDITED BY LOIS WINSTON

ACKNOWLEDGMENTS

A special thank-you to all the authors who participated in this project. It wouldn't have been possible without you.

And extra thanks to Irene Peterson, Caridad Pineiro, and Sue Viders for stepping in as proofreaders.

INTRODUCTION

A friend who's an avid reader told me recently that she chooses all her books from the bestseller lists. I don't think she's alone. Most readers gravitate toward library and bookstore front racks, home to the bestsellers and recent releases by "name" authors, never venturing beyond to the general fiction and genre sections where the majority of novels reside. All you have to do is wander around your local library or bookstore to know I'm right. With few exceptions, you won't find many readers browsing in other sections. Two of those exceptions are the racks that house cookbooks and advice books.

Over the years I've read and come to enjoy books by authors who have never made it to the front racks. I realized my friend and so many other readers were missing out on some truly wonderful books. Was there something I could do to bring more readers and authors together? And that brought me back to those racks of cookbooks and advice books because all the authors I know have three things in common, no matter what genre of fiction we write.

First, we're all often asked how to go about getting published. Before you can get published, you have to write a book worthy of publication. Everyone wants to write a book, but few people know how to go about writing one.

We're also very often asked about how we do our research (especially when we're at parties and the person asking the question—usually a guy—has had too much to drink!) How do we research our sex scenes? Have we ever actually killed someone? Do we know any real vampires?

However, there are people who seriously think authors are experts when it comes to love and relationships simply because we write about them. No matter the genre, characters have relationships with other characters in our books. Characters need chemistry to connect, whether it's the positive chemistry between friends and lovers, or the negative chemistry between a protagonist and an antagonist. We have to write believable characters that come alive for our readers. So we must be experts when it comes to relationships, right? Well, whether we're experts or not, we've all had personal relationship experiences and know what has and hasn't worked for us.

And finally, every author I know has a serious sweet tooth. Chocolate or other confections sustain us through pending deadlines, crushing rejection letters, and nasty reviews. We also often celebrate our successes—selling a book, winning a writing award, making a bestseller list, receiving a fabulous review— with decadent indulgences.

So I thought, what if I combined all three of these things authors have in common? Thus was born *Bake, Love, Write: 105 Authors Share Dessert Recipes and Advice on Love and Writing*. The goal of this book is to share our favorite dessert recipes (cakes, cookies, pies, candy, and even a few vegan and gluten-free offerings) and our best advice when it comes to relationships and writing. In this way I hope to provide you with tempting treats and sage advice, as well as introduce you to authors you may not know. Hopefully, this book will lead to expanding your reading pleasure beyond the front racks and your go-to authors.

Within the pages of *Bake, Love, Write: 105 Authors Share Dessert Recipes and Advice on Love and Writing* you'll be introduced to authors who write romance, mystery, suspense, women's fiction, fantasy, paranormals, young adult, and new adult books. (I've even included a couple of non-fiction authors for those of you who don't read fiction.) Some of the authors write sweet; others write steamy. Some write cozy; others write tense thrillers. Some are debut authors with only one published book; others are multi-published and have had long publishing careers. And yes, some are bestselling authors who may or may not be familiar to you.

Because the goal of *Bake, Love, Write: 105 Authors Share Dessert Recipes and Advice on Love and Writing* is to introduce you to authors you may not know, the book isn't set up like a typical cookbook. You won't find the desserts divided into categories. I considered listing authors alphabetically, but those of us at the end of the alphabet always got stuck at the back of the classroom, and many of us still bear the scars of those unpleasant memories. So after mulling several options, I settled on listing the authors in the order they signed on to this project.

Grab a cup of coffee or a glass of wine, settle into a comfy chair, and browse through the pages of *Bake, Love, Write: 105 Authors Share Dessert Recipes and Advice on Love and Writing.* Along the way you'll hopefully discover new favorites—both recipes and authors—in addition to gleaning some relationship and writing advice. The advice might not work for you, but it's worked for our contributors. Remember that old TV commercial for Life cereal, "Try it, you'll like it"? Mikey tried it. He liked it. You might, too. You never know.

And although the title of this book is *Bake, Love, Write: 105 Authors Share Dessert Recipes and Advice on Love and Writing,* creative people are known for thinking outside the box, and authors are no exception. Not surprisingly, some didn't quite follow the rules. That's why you'll also find a few recipes for no-bake desserts, some not-so-sweet samplings, and even a doggie dessert. You'll also find some unexpected answers to the questions on love and writing. However, just think how boring the world would be if everyone always colored within the lines.

All the recipes are presented as the authors provided them except for editorial tweaking for consistent style throughout the book. In addition, I've kept the British spelling of words from our Canadian and English authors but asked them to provide non-metric measurements. Finally, as tempting as it was, none of the recipes, other than my own submission, were tested by the editor due to her ongoing battle with an expanding waistline.

If you enjoy *Bake, Love, Write: 105 Authors Share Dessert Recipes and Advice on Love and Writing*, please consider posting a review. And if you discover some new favorite authors, please tell your friends about those authors and the books you've enjoyed. Word-of-mouth is an author's best friend, and we count on our readers to provide it.

Bon appétit!
Lois Winston

Lois Winston: Apple Bundt Cake

The only problem with this cake is that you can't stop eating it.

5 cooking apples
2 teaspoons cinnamon
2-1/4 cups sugar
1 cup butter
3 cups flour
3 teaspoons baking powder
1/2 teaspoon salt
1/3 cup orange juice
4 eggs
1-1/2 teaspoons vanilla extract
1 teaspoon almond extract
confectioner's sugar

Preheat oven to 350 degrees F.

Peel and slice apples. Place in bowl. Add cinnamon and 1/4 cup sugar. Mix to coat apples. Set aside.

Cream the butter and remaining 2 cups of sugar.

Mix all other dry ingredients together. Slowly add dry ingredients to butter/sugar mixture.

Combine eggs, juice, vanilla extract, and almond extract. Slowly add to other ingredients as you continue to mix. Batter will be thick.

Grease and flour bundt pan. Place small amount of batter in bottom of pan. Add a layer of apples. Continue layering batter and apples, with batter as last layer.

Bake for 1-1/2 hours. Cool on wire rack 15-20 minutes. Remove cake from pan. Dust with confectioner's sugar.

Lois Winston is a *USA Today* bestselling author who writes mystery, romance, romantic suspense, chick lit, women's fiction, children's chapter books, and non-fiction under her own name and her Emma Carlyle pen name. *Kirkus Reviews* dubbed her critically acclaimed Anastasia Pollack Crafting Mystery series, *"North Jersey's more mature answer to Stephanie Plum."* (She plans to have that chiseled on her tombstone!) She's received starred reviews from both *Publishers Weekly* and *Booklist*, won numerous awards for her books, received a Book of the Year nomination from *ForeWord Reviews* and was a Daphne du Maurier Award finalist.

Recent releases include *Decoupage Can Be Deadly*, the latest Anastasia Pollack Crafting Mystery; *Definitely Dead*, the first book in her new Empty Nest Mystery series, and *The Magic Paintbrush*, a children's chapter book.

After working several years for a literary agency and reading through thousands of queries and partials, Lois wrote the writing advice book *Top Ten Reasons Your Novel is Rejected*. Read more about Lois and her books at www.loiswinston.com.

What's your recipe for a lasting, loving relationship?
Space! Remember that old saying: "Absence makes the heart grow fonder; familiarity breeds contempt"? It's true. Partners need to give each other permission to "do their own thing" without creating resentment. No two people are going to have all the same interests, likes, and dislikes and shouldn't expect each other to forego things they enjoy just because the other person doesn't like doing those things. That builds up resentments over time and cause problems in a relationship.

And speaking of resentments, don't keep them bottled up inside you. That's a recipe for disaster. If something bothers you, talk about it, but do so in a non-judgmental, non-confrontational manner. Don't expect your partner to be a mind reader. (The same advice extends to relationships with friends and other family members.)

What's the best writing advice you ever received?

Every scene in your manuscript must serve a purpose, and there are only two purposes to a scene—either to advance the plot or tell the reader something she needs to know about the character(s) *at that moment.* If the scene serves neither of these purposes, it's filler, and no matter how much you love what you wrote, you need to delete it. Filler has no place in a well-written novel.

Dale Mayer: Mayer Family Unbaked Cheesecake

Makes one 12" cheesecake.

6 cups graham cracker crumbs
1-1/4 cups margarine or butter, melted
3 - 8 ounce packages cream cheese
3 cups whipping cream
1-3/4 cup icing sugar
2 packages gelatin (Knox)
1/2 cup warm water
1 cup boiling water

Mix crumbs and margarine together in 12" spring-form pan. Spread the mixture along bottom and up sides, pressing firmly.

Optional: bake crust in a 350 degree F. oven until golden brown.

Dissolve 2 packs gelatin in 1/2 cup of warm water. Add 1 cup of boiling water, and 1/2 cup whipping cream.

In blender, chunk cream cheese, add gelatin liquid and 1/2 of the sugar. Blend until well mixed. Let sit.

In another bowl, cream whipping cream and the second half of the sugar until stiff. Pour cream cheese mixture into whipping cream, stirring gently until mixed. Pour into crust. Chill until set.

Options:
Fold fresh fruit into mixture at last step or pour half the cream cheese mixture into crust, add layer of fruit, then pour remaining cream cheese mixture. Top cake with fruit puree or chocolate. Use your imagination. The possibilities are endless.

Dale Mayer is a *USA Today* bestselling author best known for her Psychic

Visions and Family Blood Ties series. Her contemporary romances are raw and full of passion and emotion, her thrillers will keep you guessing, and her romantic comedies will keep you giggling. She writes young adult fiction, adult fiction and everything in-between.

Her adult fiction includes her Psychic Vision series (*Tuesday's Child, Hide'n Go Seek, Maddy's Floor, Garden of Sorrow, Knock, Knock..., Rare Find,* and *Eyes to the Soul,*) her By Death series (*Touched by Death-Part 1, Touched by Death-Part 2, Touched by Death-*Full book, *Haunted by Death,* and *Chilled by Death,*) her Second Chances...at Love series (*Second Chances-Part 1, Second Chances-Part 2,* and *Second Chances-*Full book,) and her Charmin Marvin romantic comedy series (*Broken Protocols #1, Broken Protocols #2,* and *Broken Protocols #3,*) as well as two stand-alone novels (*It's a Dog's Life* and *SKIN.*) Read more about Dale and her books at www.dalemayer.com.

What's your recipe for a lasting, loving relationship?

All relationships have certain similarities to recipes. A new recipe, like a new relationship requires a sense of adventure and a sense of acceptance to go along with the willingness to adapt it to one's taste. A favorite recipe not used in a long time is like a relationship that's gotten comfortable but could use a bit of spice. You can add ingredients in carefree abandonment to see what you create, or you can systematically try options to make what you have even better.

It's the old favorite recipe that I love. This is the one you don't need to look up. You already know that you have all the main ingredients and if you have to substitute for a missing one, you know what is liked and what will work because you've spent a lot of time on this one already. In fact, you love it anyway it works—just like a long term loving relationship!

What's the best writing advice you ever received?

Never give up! As long as you keep putting words to paper, you will improve.

Jan Carol: Bread Pudding

My recipe comes from something my mother made when I was growing up. It's moist, and delicious with whipped cream or ice cream served on top...hot or cold.

8 slices fresh bread, torn in coarse pieces
8 eggs
1/2 cup butter, melted
2 cups sugar
2 teaspoons vanilla extract
1 teaspoon cinnamon
2 cups milk

Preheat oven to 350 degrees F.

Place bread evenly in 9" x 13" pan. Mix rest of ingredients together, and pour over bread. Bake 1 hour.

Jan Carol grew up literally on the Monterey Bay beaches. If she wasn't at home, you can bet she was on the beach. She began writing her first novel at fourteen but didn't finish it until she was twenty-four. Moving to different states, her imagination moved with her, incorporating a little bit of the places she's lived and a lot of her life's experiences in her books.

She's been married for more than thirty-nine years with six children and seventeen grandchildren and has lived in the Ozarks the last twenty-seven years. Her life is never really dull! Read more about Jan and her books at www.jancarolromancenovels.weebly.com.

What's your recipe for a lasting, loving relationship?

Give much more than you take from your spouse, significant other, friend, etc. Allow them to be what they are, as long as it isn't harming others—in other words, don't hold them back from their talents and abilities, even if it means you aren't in the picture all the time. Never take them for granted; they have needs that should be met the best we know how.

What's the best writing advice you ever received?

I write because the stories are there, wanting to come out. I had no idea what to do with them for years. I let others read them and they liked them, including my children, and they kept telling me, "Keep writing. Get your stories published." Eventually, thanks to one of my daughters, I did just that.

Meg Bellamy: Easy & Delicious Grasshopper Pie

Serves 8

25 Oreo cookies
1/4 cup butter
1/4 cup creme de menthe, white or green
2 cups heavy cream
a few drops green food coloring
1 (7.5-ounces) jar of Marshmallow Fluff

Melt butter. Crush Oreo cookies. Set aside a few crumbs. Mix the rest with melted butter. Press onto bottom and sides of a 9" pie pan, making sure not to leave any gaps on the bottom. Chill crust while preparing filling.

Gradually add creme de menthe to Marshmallow Fluff, mixing until well blended. Add green food coloring sufficient to achieve desired shade. Whip cream until soft peaks form. Fold into marshmallow mixture, blending thoroughly. Pour into pie shell. Wrap in foil and freeze until ready to serve.

Meg Bellamy has many passions. Along with her husband, her family and her books, these include language, travel, cooking, baking, knitting, and quilting. If shopping were an Olympic sport, Meg would score several gold medals. It's a good thing Meg loves to travel, since she lives in the gorgeous San Francisco Bay Area, but her daughter settled in New Jersey and her son in England. Talk about Frequent Flying! Between flights this long-time language teacher writes contemporary romance and women's fiction.

Meg enjoys looking at life and love with a good dose of humor and irony. Her single title novel, *Homecoming*, was released by The Wild Rose Press. She's currently writing two series of romantic stories—TV Tales, and Nuclear Nuptials. Her latest indie release is *Divorce by Chocolate*. Read more about Meg and her books at www.MegBellamy.com.

What's your recipe for a lasting, loving relationship?
First and foremost, pick the right partner for you.

Be romantic, and be real. There's a time and place for each quality. Sometimes romance and reality can occupy the same space and time; sometimes they can't. Don't let the romance blind you to the demands of reality, and don't let harsh doses of reality rob you of your romance. Be flexible.

Love is a gift and a blessing. It's a force of nature but is also delicate and in need of care and feeding. If you're fortunate enough to love and be loved, don't take your good fortune for granted. Nurture your love and pamper your love during the good times so that it can weather the tough times.

A sense of humor is crucial.

Focus on what you appreciate about your love, and remind yourself of these qualities when mundane annoyances make you want to grind your teeth.

Take the time to smell the roses, the coffee, or whatever floats your love boat. Did I mention that a sense of humor is essential?

What's the best writing advice you ever received?
Read, read, read. Write, write, write. Revise, revise, revise. Repeat.

It's essential to know your own style. Mine is to fill the page and then revise—a lot. Some people are more content to do a lot of planning and write such an excellent first draft that they don't require much revision. I envy them, but I realize that style doesn't work for me.

Writing is solitary, but it's also important to be part of a community that "gets" you. "Talk" with other writers—whether on-line or at meetings and conferences. Participate in the generosity of the writing community—both as a recipient and as a donor.

Stick with it and don't lose sight of your dreams!

Bobbi A. Chukran: Lavender Shortbread Cookies

This recipe is easy, and everyone loves these. It makes a great dessert to go with rose tea or as a gift for the hostess of a garden party. They freeze well, but that's usually not a problem. Makes about 3-dozen large cookies, or 4-dozen smaller ones.

3/4 cup unsalted butter
1 cup sugar
2 eggs
3/4 teaspoon vanilla extract
3 teaspoons dried lavender flowers, organic, finely chopped
1-1/2 cups all-purpose flour
2 teaspoons baking powder

Preheat oven to 375 degrees F.

Cream butter and sugar until light and fluffy. Beat in the eggs, vanilla extract, and lavender flowers. Mix well.

In another bowl, combine the flour and baking powder, then add to the lavender mixture. Stir until well blended.

Drop by teaspoonfuls onto ungreased baking sheet. Bake 8-10 minutes or until lightly brown on the edges. Cool for a minute or two, then transfer cookies to a baking rack to continue cooling.

Bobbi A. Chukran is a Texas native who loves writing stories about small-town quirky characters who just can't help but get into trouble. She's the author of an historical mystery, *Lone Star Death*, the Nameless, Texas series of short stories, and the novella, *Dye, Dyeing, Dead*. Bobbi's characters are usually interested in gardening, cooking, cats and folklore—just like she is. Bobbi has also written award-winning plays for youth. *Annierella & the (Very Awesome) Good Queen Fairy Cowmother* and *Little Red Riding Boots & Cooter Coyote (Master of Disguise)* are the latest, published by Brooklyn Publishing.

Bobbi tends a huge cottage garden of culinary herbs and old-fashioned flowers. She moons over eighty heirloom rosebushes that came with her vintage 1930s home, a never-ending source of fun DIY projects. Read more about Bobbi and her books at www.bobbichukran.com.

What's your recipe for a lasting, loving relationship?

My recipe for a loving relationship is to marry someone who likes to cook and can make good coffee, because if you're an author, you will starve otherwise. My husband of 25(!) years took numerous cooking classes before I met him. He was cruising for chicks at the time, I suspect, but the kitchen skills he picked up have come in very handy over the years.

What's the best writing advice you ever received?

I got some advice on making art years ago from a good friend of mine, Sharon Wilcox. She said, "Don't let your head think any farther than the end of your hands." I don't paint much anymore, but I do use that same advice when I'm writing. It's hard because of many distractions here, but it's good advice I try to follow.

Melissa Keir: Kuchen

This recipe for Kuchen (German Coffee Cake) came from my great-grandmother. Growing up, all the women in the family would come together to make these treats and freeze them for later. I love mine slightly warm with butter.

1 cup sugar
1/2 cup shortening melted (or melted margarine)
2 eggs
2 cups lukewarm milk
3-4 cups flour
3 packages of yeast mixed with 1/2 cup milk
1 teaspoon salt
4 cups sour cream
1/2 cup brown or granulated sugar
cinnamon

Preheat oven to 375 degrees F.

Mix 1 cup sugar, shortening, eggs, milk, flour, yeast, and salt into a stiff batter and let rise until doubled in size. Remove from bowl and separate into 5-6 greased cake pans to rise again.

Before baking, spread half the sour cream evenly over kuchen batter. Sprinkle generously with white or brown sugar. Bake until top is lightly brown.

Remove pans from oven. When almost cool, spread more sour cream, mixed with 1/2 cup sugar, over kuchen, then sprinkle with cinnamon.

The fully cooled kuchen can be frozen to be enjoyed later.

Melissa Keir has always wanted to be an author when she wasn't hoping for a career as a racecar driver. Her love of books was instilled by her mother and grandparents who were avid readers. She'd often sneak books away from them so that she could fantasize about those strong alpha males and plucky heroines. In middle school and high school, Melissa used to write sappy love poems and share them with her friends. In college her writing changed to sarcastic musings on life as well as poems with a modern twist on fairy tales, for which she won awards.

Books by Melissa include: *Second Time's the Charm* (Charming Chances #1), *Three's a Crowd* (Charming Chances #2), *Forever Love* (The Wilder Sisters #1), *Beach Desires* (The Wilder Sisters #2), *A Christmas Accident* (The Wilder Sisters #3), and *Chalkboard Romance*. Read more about Melissa and her books at www.melissakeir.com.

What's your recipe for a lasting, loving relationship?

When I met my husband, I was divorced and had some issues with trust. He made me feel like I was important. My husband sent me silly texts and emails throughout my day, just to let me know he was thinking of me. It wasn't love at first sight for us. In fact, he rubbed me the wrong way. But when I got to know his sarcastic sense of humor, I realized that he was a man who kept my brain on its toes. Hey, brains are sexy in a guy! So is a sense of humor. At least to me! And while my husband wasn't built like Hugh Jackman, his body "fit" mine. In other words, he's only a little taller than me and has strong shoulders and arms to hold me close.

However, he urged me to stand on my own feet rather than rely on another. As I said, he made me want to be a better person. I see that as love...not lust, but a deep sense of commitment and caring for another human being, someone you could spend the rest of your life with.

When I write about my heroes in my books, they have pieces of my husband in them. Whether it's their caring nature, or the way they push the heroine to be stronger...those things are little hints at the deep love I share with my husband and what I want for my characters. After all, isn't a happily ever after the goal of every romance writer?

What's the best writing advice you ever received?

The best writing advice is to never give up. I had two publishing houses close before and after my first book was published. It was devastating and I felt that I would never get to share my story with readers. A good friend and fellow author encouraged me to submit my manuscript to one of the publishing houses she was with. Because I didn't give up, my first book was published and my story, *Forever Love*, was born.

The advice of never giving up also fits when you get stuck. Writer's block happens. You have a fab idea and the story begins but somewhere along the way, you can't find the next perfect words. Days of avoiding writing draw into weeks. But you shouldn't give up. Write every day. Even if it's not the perfect words, perfect story, or perfect feeling, by writing you are putting those skills to use and soon your block will fall away.

Never gives up applies to life in a bigger sense. We've all faced struggles...but when we give up, failure happens. When we keep pushing through, when we keep trying, when we never give up...we can be triumphant.

Amy Gamet: Butter Pecan Cookies

8 ounces unsalted butter
3/4 cup sugar
3/4 teaspoon salt
1-1/2 teaspoons pure vanilla extract
1 large egg yolk
2 cups flour
1 cup unsalted pecans, very finely chopped or lightly ground in food processor
1/2 to1 cup chopped toffee pieces (optional)

Preheat oven to 325 degrees F.

Blend the butter, sugar, salt and vanilla extract in a mixer until creamy. Add egg yolk and blend again. Add flour, finely chopped pecans and toffee pieces, then mix until just blended.

Drop by spoonfuls onto a baking sheet or roll into a log and refrigerate for several hours. Then roll out dough and use cookie cutters.

Bake until edges just begin to brown, 15-20 minutes depending on shape and thickness.

Amy Gamet is the *USA Today* bestselling author of the Love and Danger romantic suspense series (*Meant for Her, The One Who Got Away, Artful Deception,* and *Meghan's Wish*) and the Moon Lake contemporary romance series (*Treasure on Moon Lake.*) She has three kids, a super-supportive husband, a slightly stinky and poorly trained dog, and an ancient calico cat that doesn't like people. Her house is in a perpetual state of disarray because she'd rather write about imaginary people than wash the socks of real ones. Read more about Amy and her books at www.amygamet.com.

What's your recipe for a lasting, loving relationship?
Don't crack eggs when you're angry. Remember that flour is always going to

get on the counter and the floor and the front of your shirt, so don't blame the flour for being messy. When your arm gets tired of stirring, be grateful you have someone to share the work. Make sure you both clean up the dishes sometimes, and maybe even help him when it's his turn because it goes a lot faster that way. Surprise him with cupcakes on silly anniversaries, and put the extra frosting in the refrigerator, even though you know he'll sneak inside and eat it before the sun goes down. And most important for a lasting relationship, make sure to preheat the oven!

What's the best writing advice you ever received?

Leave something to your reader's imagination. If I tell you my hero walked into a crowded, narrow diner, you immediately have a visual, from the booths to the counter to the display case for deserts, maybe even a waitress and what she's wearing. If I were to describe each of those things, it actually prevents the reader from investing in the text in the same manner as a few key descriptive words.

Kristy Tate: Christmas Corn

2 packages of microwave popcorn, popped
1 cup of Wilton's Milk Chocolate Melts
1 cup of Wilton's White Chocolate Melts
3 smashed candy canes

Pop corn according to directions. Line a cookie sheet with tinfoil and spread popcorn in a single layer over the foil. Pick out all of the unpopped kernels.

Melt the chocolate in the microwave for one minute, or until smooth when stirred. Pour over the corn. Sprinkle the candy canes over the top. Let cool.

Kristy Tate writes romance dashed with mystery and humor. Her debut novel, *Stealing Mercy*, was on Amazon's top 100 list of historical romance for more than fifteen weeks and spent two weeks as number one. Her participation in the *Christmas on Main Street* Anthology, an Amazon #1 bestseller, inspirational romance, made her an Amazon top 100 author. Her novel, *The Rhyme's Library*, was a 2013 Kindle Review semi-finalist. Her other titles include, *Beyond the Fortuneteller's Tent, Beyond the Hollow, Stuck With You, A Ghost of a Second Chance, Losing Penny, Rescuing Rita,* and *A Light in the Christmas Café.*

Kristy studied English literature at Brigham Young University and at BYU's International Center in London. Although a long time resident of Orange County, California, where she lives with her family, Kristy's heart belongs in her hometown of Arlington, Washington, AKA Rose Arbor—the fictional setting of her popular Rose Arbor series. Read more about Kristy and her books at www.kristystories.blogspot.com.

What's your recipe for a lasting, loving relationship?
Writing.

Here I am when I'm not writing:

Carol drops by with a pan of brownies. She looks like a teenager in that halter-top. She says, "I brought these for your husband to thank him for helping me fix that broken window." I say, "Thank you," but I'm thinking I really wish she'd wear more clothes. I wonder what she was wearing when Larry was at her house, and for how long was he there? I can't compare myself to her—I had six kids and she has a dog. Maybe my abs would look like hers if I had countless hours to spend at the gym. Does she work out at the same gym as Larry? Why does she call him all the time? He doesn't even like brownies. But I love them. I bet she knows that. She knows that I'm going to eat this entire pan of brownies because now I'm depressed and one or two or five brownies aren't going to matter because I'm going to be divorced and fat.

Here I am when I'm writing:
The doorbell rings, but I don't hear it because somehow Mercy has to stop Eloise from going on a drive with horrid Mr. Steele. What can she do—should she confide in Eloise? In the real world, my dog is pawing at me. No. Eloise is a blabbermouth. She can't be trusted. My dog knows someone has come to the door, and she pulls at my sock with her teeth. I reluctantly investigate and find brownies on my front porch with a thank-you note from Carol, that darling girl from across the street. I consider the brownies and inspiration hits— Mercy will bake Eloise a pie laced with a draught that will make her sleep through her rendezvous with Steele. I put the brownies on the counter and save them for when Larry comes home. I hurry back to Mercy, Eloise and Mr. Steele, wondering how to make a sleeping draught.

(FYI- Neighbor Carol is fictional, used to make a point about my own lunacy and not a commentary on my highly respectable, modestly clothed and admirable neighbors or my good husband who always lets me eat more than my fair share of brownies.)

What's the best writing advice you ever received?
Don't fight. If you're fuming and rummaging through your head trying to formulate the perfect stinging comeback, you won't be in tune with your story or characters. It's impossible, for me at least, to feel in sync with my writing if I'm too busy mentally constructing closing arguments. I'm not advocating

being a pansy; I'm just saying learn to be a peacemaker. It'll help you be a better writer (and a nicer person.)

Take Notes. Truth really is stranger than fiction, and I like to look for what I call novel fodder. Strange and incredible things happen every day. People, especially children, say amazingly clever things. Novel fodder happens right outside my door. For example, once while attending a school board meeting at the beach club, as I listened to a board member give a speech full of lies, a mother duck and a line of her babies wandered through the crowd, quacking. It was such a funny contraposition I used it in *A Library in Rhyme*. So, go ahead and eavesdrop. And take notes. Something bizarre is bound to happen.

Don't try to be like Jack or Marylou. Jack and Marylou belong to my writing group and are very poetic writers. I love their use of language. Their prose is lyrical and beautiful. Their sentences are long. I confess, I fell into the trap of trying to mimic their style. It didn't work. I just had a slew of run-on sentences. One of the best bits of writing advice I ever received was this: write like you're telling your best friend a story. If your best friend is Cormac McCarthy, go ahead and wax poetic, but if not...be yourself.

Terry Shames: Momo's German Chocolate Cake

My grandmother loved all things lemon or custard, but all the rest of her family craved chocolate. This was one of their favorites.

1 cup shortening*
3-1/4 cups sugar
2 -1/2 cups cake flour
1 package German chocolate, melted in 1/2 cup hot water
1 cup buttermilk
4 teaspoons vanilla extract
4 egg whites, beaten stiff
2 egg whites
7 egg yolks
1 teaspoon baking soda
1 can condensed milk
2 tablespoons butter
1 cup coconut
1-1/2 cups pecans, chopped
1 stick margarine
2 squares unsweetened Baker's chocolate
1 egg, beaten well
2 cups confectioner's sugar

Preheat over to 350 degrees F.

For cake, cream together shortening and 2 cups sugar. Add 4 egg yolks one at a time, beating after each addition. Add 3/4 cup buttermilk, alternately with flour. Mix baking soda in remaining buttermilk and add to mixture. Add melted German chocolate and 1 teaspoon vanilla extract. Fold in the 4 stiffly beaten egg whites. Pour batter into 3 or 4 round layer cake pans. Bake for 30 minutes. Cool.

For filling, place remaining three egg yolks, remaining sugar, 2 egg whites, 1 teaspoon vanilla extract, condensed milk, and butter in top of double boiler.

24

Cook until thick. Remove from heat. Fold in coconut and 1/2 cup pecans. Place filling between layers of cake.

For icing, melt margarine and unsweetened chocolate squares together. Add 1 beaten egg, 2 teaspoons vanilla extract, confectioner's sugar, and 1 cup chopped pecans.

*Shortening was originally lard. Eventually hydrogenated vegetable oil took its place. To reduce trans-fats you can use margarine or shortening formulated to be low in trans fats. Butter is not a good substitute.

Terry Shames is the author of the bestselling Samuel Craddock series, set in the fictitious town of Jarrett Creek, Texas. Books in the series include *A Killing at Cotton Hill*, *The Last Death of Jack Harbin*, *Dead Broke in Jarrett Creek*, and *A Deadly Affair at Bobtail Ridge*.

Terry grew up in Texas and has great affection for the town where her grandparents lived, the model for Jarrett Creek. She now lives in Berkeley, California with her husband and two rowdy terriers. Read more about Terry and her books at www.Terryshames.com.

What's your recipe for a lasting, loving relationship?
1 heaping cup of mutual respect
2 cups sense of humor
1/2 cup compromise
1 cup kindness
1/2 cup self-respect
1/2 cup variety

Mix first four ingredients until well blended. Add self-respect as needed. Sprinkle with variety. This recipe is meant to be grilled in the sunshine, baked on rainy days, and toasted over a warm fire when it's cold. On gloomy days it can be warmed over as many times as needed. Can be used in the home, out and about in the neighborhood, or when traveling. Good any time of day or night. If you run out of any ingredient, ask loved ones to replenish.

The results are especially delicious when life gets hard, when disappointment hits, or when in-laws overstay their visit. It can be shared with special friends, new friends, and relatives. Those who share the recipe freely will find that it expands the more it is used. Children love it and will want to share the recipe with everyone they know.

Warning when used with children: Use of this recipe may result in having a houseful of happy kids.

What's the best writing advice you ever received?

A few years ago writers Sophie Littlefield and Cornelia Read held a weekend workshop for aspiring mystery writers. They arranged for every aspect of mystery writing to be addressed—from an in-depth talk by experienced San Francisco cops, to craft sessions, to an agent Q & A. On the last day Sophie gave a pep talk. She had written several books before she signed her first publishing contract, and she said that things changed for her when she made a heartfelt commitment to being a successful writer.

She said commitment means turning down "fun" with friends in order to spend extra time writing. It means doing your homework in terms of craft and market potential. But most deeply she said it means digging deep inside and finding what only you have to offer as a writer.

I had heard this advice before: look at the bookshelves and find out what wasn't there; come up with a different gimmick, a different slant on things. But nothing struck me the way Sophie's talk did.

A couple of weeks later I sat down to let my inner voice tell me what I had that no one else had. As if by magic a vision came to me of a man sitting on a porch in a rocking chair. A woman walked up the steps and told him that a good friend of his had been murdered. I saw the scene as clearly as if it were on a movie screen. Samuel Craddock had announced himself to me.

From the beginning I knew something special had happened. It took only two months to complete the manuscript, and another month to edit it. It seemed like magic, but I believe it never would have happened without the impassioned speech from Sophie the last day of that workshop.

Barbara Phinney: Rhubarb Meringue Cake

1-1/4 cups all–purpose flour
1-1/2 cups sugar
1-1/2 teaspoons baking powder
1/2 teaspoon salt
3/4 cup milk
1/3 cup shortening
1 egg
2 teaspoons vanilla extract
2 cups chopped rhubarb*
5 egg whites
1/2 cup sugar
1/2 teaspoon cream of tartar

Preheat oven to 350 degrees F.

*Only use the fleshy red stems. Some rhubarb is sold with the leaves still on. Rhubarb leaves are poisonous.

Combine flour, 1 cup sugar, baking powder, salt, milk, shortening, egg, and 1 teaspoon vanilla extract. Beat on low mixer speed, scraping bowl constantly, for 30 seconds. Beat again at high speed for three minutes, scraping the bowl occasionally.

Pour batter into a 9-10" cake pan. Do not use an 8" pan as the addition of rhubarb will make it overflow. Spread the rhubarb on top of the batter. Do not mix. Bake for 45 minutes or until knife comes out clean from the center. Allow to cool.

Meanwhile, beat the egg whites until foamy. Add remaining sugar. Beat until soft peaks form. Add cream of tartar and remaining vanilla extract. Beat until stiff peaks form. Spread meringue on top of cake.
Brown meringue in 400 degree F oven until peaks and edges are brown. Cool

before serving. Meringue can weep after a day or two, but it still tastes good!

Barbara Phinney is a *USA Today* bestselling author who retired from the military to raise her two children and soon turned her creativity toward writing. Nearly twenty years later, she's published with Harlequin, and is also taking the plunge into the self-publishing pool, with *Deadly Trust*, set in the shadow of the bridge to Prince Edward Island, on the warm beaches that inspire her.

Barbara lives in Eastern Canada with her husband and also writes mysteries and sci-fi under her Georgina Lee pen name. Her latest romance is *Protected by the Warrior*, while Georgina Lee's latest is *Cape of Secrets*. *Death on the Ocean Floor* will be a November 2014 release, and *Sheltered by the Warrior* will be available February 2015. Read more about Barbara and her books at www.barbaraphinney.com.

What's your recipe for a lasting, loving relationship?

Patience, adaptability and total devotion. Take the time to spend one-on-one together. Find common loves and do them together. Laugh with your loved one often. And don't forget to hold hands.

What's the best writing advice you ever received?

Write. Then write some more. Edit, and keep writing. Develop a thick skin and remember: only the Ten Commandments were written in stone. Your stuff can be edited.

Kitsy Clare: Lucky in Love Sweet Fruit Roll

Makes a 12" pastry roll.

2 cups flour
pinch of salt
1/2 cup sugar
7 tablespoons butter, chilled and cut into small pieces
1 egg yolk
approximately 5 tablespoons white wine or water
1 teaspoon vanilla extract
1/3 grated lemon zest (optional)
1/3 cup raisins, golden or dark
1/2 cup walnuts
2/3 cup chopped almonds
3/4 cup plum or apricot jam
10 dried figs, chopped
3/4 cup red wine
1/4 teaspoon cinnamon
1/8 teaspoon ground cloves
1/4 teaspoon cardamom
1 beaten egg
dashes of confectioner's sugar

Preheat oven to 350 degrees F.

Combine butter and sugar in a mixing bowl until creamy. Add eggs, water (or 5 tablespoons wine) and vanilla extract. Mixing after each addition. Add flour and salt. Blend until dough is consistent but soft. Don't over-mix! Can chill in fridge for a while if you like.

To make the fruit filling, cut the figs into medium-sized sections. In saucepan on low heat, heat wine and jam to a boil, then add figs. Cook for about three minutes. Add nuts and spices. Simmer another 6-8 minutes until everything is mixed in. Remove from stove and stir.

Knead dough on a floured surface. Roll into a long rectangle shape. Place fruit filling in center, and fold dough over. Seal the sides and ends by making gentle thumb-presses around the edges. You can cut a few little horizontal air holes on the top to facilitate cooking. Brush beaten egg on top, then dust with confectioner's sugar. Bake 30-35 minutes or until golden brown.

Kitsy Clare lives in Manhattan. A romantic at heart, she loves writing about the sexy intrigue of the city and of the art world, both of which she knows well. *Model Position*, her new adult novella, is about an artist and her friends. *Living in a Bookworld* says: *"Beautifully written! We learn things about art & painting. A colorful story from a promising author."* The next in The Art of Love series, *Private Internship* launches fall 2014 with Inkspell.

Kitsy loves to travel and teach workshops. She also writes YA as Catherine Stine. Her futuristic thriller, *Ruby's Fire* was a YA finalist in the Next Generation Indie book awards. *Fireseed One*, its companion novel, was a finalist in YA and Sci-Fi in the USA News International Book Awards, and an Indie Reader notable. Her YA horror, *Dorianna*, launches fall 2014 with Evernight Teen. Read more about Kitsy/Catherine and her books at www.catherinestine.com.

What's your recipe for a lasting, loving relationship?
My hubby and I have been married a while now, so we must be doing something right! I'm sure what has sustained us is that we are very good friends, and we share a love of art, music and gardening. We are also both writers, and we help each other through writing snags and rough drafts.

Laughter is important, too. We have a similarly quirky sense of humor, and we often bring up running joke lines and funny memories. Some of them are much more humorous now than they were when they were happening! You know what I mean? You can't take yourself too seriously. It's much more fun to chuckle together.

What's the best writing advice you ever received?
Here are lines from various mentors that never leave me. They play in my

mind when I need them most: *Paint the rough brushstroke of the scene. Entertain, always. Write from beyond what you know, into what you sense. Put one strong sentence after the other, one strong chapter after the other.*

Finally, the best way to learn how to write well is to read, voraciously.

Raine English: Grandma's Slovenian Apple Strudel

3 cups all-purpose flour
2 eggs
1/4 cup shortening
3/4 cup lukewarm water or a little more (to keep dough on soft side)
3/4 teaspoon white vinegar
1-1/2 teaspoons salt
1/2 cup butter, melted
2-1/2 lbs. apples, peeled and sliced thin
1 to 1-1/2 cups sugar (depending on how sweet your apples are)
1/2 cup raisins (dark or white)
1/2 cup crushed corn flakes (or cracker crumbs)
cinnamon (to taste)

Preheat oven to 400 degrees F.

Place raisins in hot water for a few minutes to plump. Dry them well.

Mix shortening and flour as you would for pie dough. Add eggs and mix thoroughly. Add vinegar to the lukewarm water, then add to the mixture and mix well. Beat the dough with your hand until it falls away from the bowl and is bubbly and light. Knead on a floured cloth a few minutes until nice and smooth. Grease with 1/4 cup melted butter and let rest about a half an hour, well covered in a warm place.

Cover a large table with a large cloth; sprinkle lightly with flour. Place the dough on the middle of the table and gently start stretching the dough from the center, then moving all around evenly until thin as tissue paper and hangs 1-2" below the table. Trim off thick ends.

Brush 1/4 cup melted butter all over dough with a pastry brush. Sprinkle lightly with sugar. Let stand until it almost dries but do not let it dry out. This will cause the dough to crack. It must be soft enough to roll smoothly.

Spread apples and corn flake crumbs (or cracker crumbs) evenly over dough, leaving 4" all around without filling, then add raisins, cinnamon, sugar and pats of butter (randomly placed) Don't over-butter.

Grease pan with butter. Take the end of your cloth and roll entire dough and filling. Cut into strips the size of your pan. Put a little butter over the top of strips, then seal ends to keep juices in. Bake for about 40 minutes. If browning too fast, cover loosely with foil.

Raine English always wanted to be a writer. She began her career as a journalist, but writing romance novels was her passion. Her stories have won many awards, including finaling in the Romance Writers of America Golden Heart and winning the Daphne du Maurier Award. She enjoys writing both adult and young adult romances, eerie Gothic historical novels, and sweet contemporary short stories.

When not behind her computer, you can find her reading, usually something involving the supernatural. She lives in New England with her family and two dogs. Read more about Raine and her books at www.RaineEnglish.com.

What's your favorite recipe for a lasting, loving relationship?
2 cups honesty
1 cup communication
1/4 cup appreciation
a pinch of devotion, respect, and passion
a dash of fun

Mix together, then sprinkle with some kindness and love. Bake until done.

Suggestion: Never discuss finances on an empty stomach. Serve dessert first.

What's the best writing advice you ever received?
Write every day. You won't succeed if you don't put pen to paper and produce on a regular basis.

Cathryn Cade: Best Ever Banana Bars

As addictive as great romance!

3/4 cup butter
2/3 cup sugar
2/3 cup brown sugar, packed
1 large egg or 2 small eggs
1 teaspoon vanilla extract
2 large ripe bananas
2 cups flour (may use all purpose, or up to 1/2 cup whole wheat)
2 teaspoons baking powder
1/2 teaspoon salt
6 ounces chocolate chips, semi-sweet or milk chocolate

Preheat oven to 350 degrees F.

Cream together butter, sugars, egg, and vanilla extract until smooth and fluffy. Add bananas, beating on slow/medium speed until well mixed.

Stir together flour, baking powder, and salt. Add to wet ingredients, beating until combined. Stir in chocolate chips.

Spread evenly in greased 10" x 15" baking pan. Bake for 25 minutes.

Cool, cut into squares.

Cathryn Cade writes red-hot sci-fi, paranormal and contemporary romance from the lake country of North Idaho, where she lives with her husband and a golden retriever named Copper. When she's not loosing alpha males on the unsuspecting galaxy, Cathryn loves to boat, bike, gallery hop and cook. Read more about Cathryn and her books at www.cathryncade.com.

What's your recipe for a lasting, loving relationship?
Having been married happily for thirty-four years, I can say a good marriage

needs healthy doses of humor, tolerance of each other's foibles, and staying busy with activities you both enjoy—and keeping that desire kindled.

What's the best writing advice you ever received?

To write what I want to read. That's how I began and how I continue to write...and readers seem to want to read that, too!

Haley Whitehall: Apple Pie

7/8 cup sugar

2/3 teaspoon cinnamon (I use 1/2 teaspoon cinnamon and a heavy 1/4)

2 tablespoons flour

5 cups apples, peeled and sliced

1 tablespoon margarine or butter, melted

2 pie crusts

Preheat oven to 425 degrees F.

Mix sugar, cinnamon, and flour in bowl. Add to sliced apples and stir together. Add melted margarine or butter.

Place one pie crust in 10" pie pan. Pour apples into pan. Stretch second pie crust over apples, sealing edges. Cut vent holes in crust.

Bake for 30 minutes. Lower the temperature to 350 degrees and cover crust with foil. Bake an additional 15-20 minutes.

Haley Whitehall has wanted to be a writer since she was four years old. She attended Central Washington University and majored in her other favorite subject: history. She has social studies and library endorsements. Now she pairs her two passions into writing historical fiction set in the United States in the nineteenth century. The Civil War is her favorite era.

Haley lives in Washington State where she enjoys all four seasons and the surrounding wildlife. When she's not researching or writing, she plays with her cats, watches the Western and History Channels, and goes antiquing. She's hoping to build a time machine to help her with research. A good book, a cup of coffee, and a view of the mountains make her happy.

Haley's historical romances include *Midnight Caller*, *Midnight Heat*, *Midnight Kiss*, *Soldier in Her Lap*, and *Wild and Tender Care*. Read more about her and her books at www.haleywhitehall.com.

What's your recipe for a lasting, loving relationship?

A lasting, loving relationship is based on mutual respect. I believe a relationship requires an equal investment from both partners. Don't go into a relationship with your eyes closed. We all have flaws and need to accept that fact. I think most people would agree that trying to drastically change your partner never works; it only drives him away.

Communication is key. When a problem arises you need to talk it out, don't hold the anger in and let is fester. Too many relationships are ruined from misunderstandings. Also, it's important to learn patience and the art of compromise. I think shared interests are important or at the least the willingness to spend time with your partner doing things he enjoys. If you like to go antiquing and your partner likes to go fishing, you could agree to spend a day once a month doing those things together. Equally important is time away from your partner. We need alone time or time out with friends in order to recharge our batteries and maintain a healthy relationship.

Don't sweat the small stuff. Only worry about what is truly important. Even if you are bogged down with work, make time for your partner. Date nights can save a marriage.

What's the best writing advice you ever received?

I guess the best advice I've received was that it was okay to be an author. Don't hold back on your dreams. Instead of talking about writing a book, sit down and do it. Writing is a very personal and rewarding experience. There will always be doubters. Some people will think you are wasting your time, but if the writing fire burns within you, fan the flames. Don't let the naysayers put it out. Surround yourself with a supportive group of fellow creative minds.

Here's a little more specific advice that I think is worth sharing: Writing to trends is never a good idea as trends change quickly. Write the story that is in your heart. Readers will know if you are faking it. If you fall in love with the book you are writing, if you feel like the characters are so real you've known them all your life, then your readers will, too.

Writing should be an emotional journey for both the writer and the reader. If your moods don't change as you write the highs and lows in your plot arc, then you're probably not digging deeply enough. And don't be afraid to take chances.

Shilpa Mudiganti: Sooji ka halwa (Semolina Pudding)

This is a traditional sweet Indian dessert made especially as a divine offering to Hindu Gods after specific rituals/festivals. This is not to say that it can't be or isn't enjoyed at other occasions. It's easy-to-make and extremely delicious!

1 cup semolina
1/4 cup ghee (clarified butter)
3-4 teaspoons ground cardamom
1/2 cup assorted nuts
3/4 cup sugar
hot water (or hot milk if desired)

Heat a small amount of ghee in a non-stick pan. Lightly fry the assorted nuts till they are light brown. Remove the nuts and set aside.

Add some more ghee in the pan and slowly add the semolina. Keep mixing until semolina is well coated with the ghee. Fry until light brown. Add the sugar and hot water (or milk) and mix gently. Add the cardamom powder and nuts and continue stirring gently. Once all water is absorbed, turn off heat and keep covered for few minutes. Serve hot.

Shilpa Mudiganti Mirza is an entrepreneur, author, and founder of Inkspell Publishing, an independent publishing house of romance and fantasy fiction, based out of Michigan, USA. She started the publishing house in 2012 when she published her first romance novel, *Always You*. She expanded the company to include over twenty books and eighteen authors within the first year. The company continues to expand under her business partner since she sold her stake in 2014. She has now moved on to her next venture, Picmela.com, a social media platform for photographers to be launched by the end of 2014.

Shilpa is always on the lookout for new online outlets to help authors and readers and blogs on The Good Villain, an author enabling resource she launched in 2013. When she has spare time, she blogs, connects with her readers, and spends time with her loving husband. Shilpa lives in Ridgefield Park, New Jersey. Read more about her at www.shilpamudiganti.com.

What's your recipe for a lasting, loving relationship?

Having married my college boyfriend of eight years, five years of which were long distance, we strongly believe a mix of trust, openness and constant dialogue an excellent recipe for a loving and lasting relationship.

What's the best writing advice you ever received?

Short sentences and dialogues that move the story forward! But more importantly, write your heart out and only then, worry about editing.

Melinda Curtis: Molten Chocolate Lava Cake

This recipe serves 6 and only takes 15 minutes to prepare.

8 ounces bittersweet chocolate, coarsely chopped
3/4 cup butter plus 2 tablespoons
3 eggs
3 egg yolks
1/3 cup granulated sugar
1 teaspoon vanilla extract
1 tablespoon all-purpose flour
confectioner's sugar
unsweetened cocoa powder

Preheat the oven to 425 degrees F.

Grease six 8-10 ounce ramekins, soufflé dishes, or custard cups with 2 tablespoons butter. Place ramekins in a 15" x 10" x 1" baking pan. Set aside.

In a small saucepan, combine the chocolate and remainder of butter. Cook over low heat, stirring constantly, until the chocolate melts. Remove pan from heat. Set aside.

In a large mixing bowl, beat the eggs, egg yolks, granulated sugar, and vanilla extract with an electric mixer on high speed 8-10 minutes, or until thick and a lemon color. Fold 1/3 of the chocolate mixture into the egg mixture. Fold remaining chocolate mixture and flour into egg mixture. Spoon about 2/3 cup batter into each prepared ramekin.

Bake about 12 minutes or until cake edges feel firm. Cool in ramekins on a wire rack 2-3 minutes. Using a knife, loosen the cakes from the sides of the ramekins. Place onto dessert plates. Sift with powdered sugar and cocoa powder. Serve immediately.

Melinda Curtis writes the Harmony Valley series of sweet romances for the

Harlequin Heartwarming line. Brenda Novak says: *"Season of Change has found a place on my keeper shelf."* Melinda also writes independently published, hotter romances as Mel Curtis. Jayne Ann Krentz says of *Blue Rules*: *"Sharp, sassy, modern version of a screwball comedy from Hollywood's Golden Age except a lot hotter."*

Melinda is married to her college sweetheart, and has three kids in college. She follows the NFL because one young quarterback is from her hometown, and follows Duke basketball because Mr. Curtis has a man crush on Coach K. Her latest releases are *Gemma Rules*, book 3.5 in The Hollywood Rules series, and *Season of Change*, book 3 in the Harmony Valley series. Keep an eye out for her upcoming release from the Hollywood Rules series, *Breaking the Rules*, a hot novella featuring Jack and Viv's story. Read more about Melinda and her books at www.melindacurtis.net.

What's your recipe for a lasting, loving relationship?
Honesty. Be honest when your significant other has done something that makes you happy, annoys you, or threatens your equilibrium. If you can't be honest with each other, what are you basing your relationship on?

What's the best writing advice you ever received?
Just write the story. You don't need fancy words or clever phrases. You just need to get it down on paper, not angst about a clever way to say it. Paula Eykelhof told me that when she edited my first book. Words to live by (although I still try to be clever and write fresh.)

Jessa Slade: Mint Chocolate "Deadline" Brownies

When deadlines loom—whether it's a book due or a block party tomorrow— Deadline Brownies are super fast and sooo tasty.

family-size brownie mix (I recommend Duncan Hines Chewy Fudge Brownies. Yes, that's a lot of brownies, but I *need* a lot of brownies, especially when I'm on deadline!)
3 tablespoons softened butter
1-1/2 cups powdered sugar
3/4 teaspoon mint extract (use high-quality extract; it makes a difference)
2 tablespoons milk
2 tablespoons butter
1/2 cup chocolate chips or chopped chocolate (I recommend Trader Joe's Pound-Plus Dark Chocolate Bar. Because you can't ever have enough pounds of chocolate when you are on deadline!)

Preheat oven according to directions on brownie mix.

Prepare brownie mix according to directions for "fudge like" brownies.

While brownies cool, prepare mint frosting. (The mint layer is great because when you're on deadline and you can't waste time brushing your teeth, you can just eat a mint brownie!) Use a hand mixer to mix softened butter, powdered sugar, mint extract, and milk into thick, smooth frosting. Slather over cooled brownies. Lick beaters.

Refrigerate the mint-frosted brownie to set up while you mix the chocolate layer.

In a double boiler or microwave, *gently* and carefully melt the remaining butter and chocolate together. Don't overheat chocolate. You shouldn't smell chocolate when it's heating; if you do, you're losing the flavor. Spread the melted mixture over the mint layer.

Gorge! I mean...share and enjoy!

Jessa Slade writes paranormal romance, urban fantasy romance, and science fiction romance—basically anything dark, mysterious, and sexy. She also writes hot contemporary romance as Jenna Dales. When she isn't writing, she bakes, gardens, beads, and walks the dog twice a day, rain or shine. She lives in the Pacific Northwest with her very own moody, broody, bad boy, rock star lover who does all the cooking. Yup, she's living the dream! Read more about Jessa at www.jessaslade.com and www.jennadales.com.

What's your recipe for a lasting, loving relationship?

Romance novels have a lot of conflict. Often the main character starts out at odds with the love interest. They spat and spark and snark. Real life can be like this, too! But the key—just as in a romance novel—is that a shared goal and mutual trust bind our lovers together. We like to focus on the "good parts," the pure lust and true love, but conflict is inevitably around the corner, whether it's a demonic monster or who forgot to take out the garbage. But the other C words—communication, compromise, and commitment—help us win through to our Happily Ever After.

What's the best writing advice you ever received?

Just write! The best way to start writing is to write. The best way to overcome writer's block is to write. The best way to get published is to write. The best way to get better at writing is to write. The best way to discover your personal themes is to write. I think the key to everything must be...to create it! And then drizzle chocolate on it ;-)

Jasmine Haynes: Hot Chocolate Pudding Cake

This is one of my favorite recipes my mother made when I was a child. On our birthdays we were allowed to choose our dessert, and mine was always Hot Chocolate Pudding Cake.

1 cup cake flour

2 teaspoons baking powder

1/2 teaspoon salt

1/2 cup sugar

4 tablespoons cocoa

1/2 cup milk

1 teaspoon vanilla extract

2 tablespoons melted shortening

1/2 cup chopped nuts (optional)

1/2 cup brown sugar

1-3/4 cups hot water

grated orange rind (optional)

Preheat oven to 350 degrees F.

Sift flour, baking powder, and salt. Add sugar, 2 tablespoons cocoa, and nuts. Add milk, vanilla extract, and shortening. Stir lightly and pour into 1-1/2 quart casserole.

In a small bowl beat together 2 tablespoons cocoa, brown sugar, hot water, and orange rind. Pour over uncooked batter. Bake for 45 minutes. As the pudding bakes, the sauce will become rich and fudgy around the cake. Top with whipped cream if desired.

Jasmine Haynes is the *NY Times* and *USA Today* bestselling author of over thirty-five classy, sensual romance tales. Look for *Pleasing Mr. Sutton*, the fifth book in her sexy West Coast series. Jasmine is also the author of the award-winning Max Starr psychic mystery series. And don't miss her writing as Jennifer Skully, KOD Daphne du Maurier award-winning author of contemporary romance, bringing you poignant tales peopled with hilarious characters that will make you laugh and make you cry. *Can't Forget You* is her new Cottonmouth adventure.

Other books by Jasmine include her Jackson Brothers Trilogy, Open Invitation Trilogy, West Coast series, Wives and Neighbors, Let's Misbehave duo, Fortune Hunter Trilogy, DeKnight Trilogy, Courtesans Trilogy, Cottonmouth series, and Max Starr series. Read more about Jasmine/Jennifer and her books at www.jasminehaynes.com.

What's your recipe for a lasting, loving relationship?

I've been married thirty years, and my recipe for a lasting, loving relationship is communication, compromise, and forgiveness. Don't yell; talk it out. Don't attack, but say your piece. Compromise. Both of you have to give and take. Sometimes you'll have to give up a little and sometimes your lover will. Sometimes you'll make mistakes, say terrible things, or do something bad. You'll want forgiveness, and remember to forgive your lover as well for any transgressions. Don't hold grudges. It'll hurt both of you in the end.

Notice how I keep saying "lover." That's because there's one more ingredient: lots of loving sex. Touch is communication. Desire is communication. Let your lover know how you feel with your body as well as your soul.

What's the best writing advice you ever received?

The best writing advice I ever received was to never give up. It took me a long time to get published, but I wanted it more than anything. I joined a great group of writers at RWA, and that's what I learned there. Keep going; don't give up. Improve your writing, learn your craft, network, and never let anyone bring you down with unconstructive criticism. Believe in yourself, and you won't give up.

Jill Blake: Italian Biscuit Bars

12 tablespoons butter
2 cups sugar
6 eggs
2 tablespoons vanilla extract or rum extract
2-3/4 cups flour
1-1/2 teaspoons baking powder

Preheat oven to 350 degrees F.

Cream butter and sugar together. Beat in eggs. Add remaining ingredients and beat two minutes.

Spread mixture onto greased and floured cookie sheet. Bake 18-19 minutes.

Cut into bars.

Jill Blake, a native of Philadelphia, now lives in Southern California with her husband and three children. During the day, she's a physician with a busy medical practice. At night, she pens steamy contemporary romances. Read more about Jill and her books at www.jillblake.blogspot.com.

What's your recipe for a lasting, loving relationship?
Listen to your partner. Take an interest in the things that are important to him: his work, hobbies, friends.

Carve out time for yourself. Continue to cultivate and pursue your own interests. Having something you're passionate about (besides your partner!) gives you something to talk about.

Don't expect to change your partner, and don't sweat the small stuff. There's a reason you fell in love—remind yourself of that reason when his socks miss the hamper *yet again*.

The *way* you say something is often more important than *what* you say. Be gentle. Comment on the behavior, not the person.

Follow the magic ratio: you need five positive interactions for every negative one.

Periodically reassess your relationship and make adjustments. Nothing in life remains static. Money, children, illness can all impact your relationship. Be aware of the stressors, communicate your concerns, and work together to adapt to changing circumstances.

Non-verbal communication is important. Hug, kiss, have sex. Even if you need to schedule it.

Laugh together. It really is the best medicine.

What's the best writing advice you ever received?

If we waited for the perfect time to have children, no one would ever procreate. Same goes for writing. Don't wait for the perfect time or idea. Just pick up your pen or open your laptop and *WRITE!*

Daryl Devore: Popcorn Balls

My favourite recipe for the holidays is a mess maker. We started this when my daughter was four or five years old and it has had several variations since we first attempted it. Also, several disasters and several moments of hysterical laughter. Safety suggestion: remove all pets from the area. Lock cats and dogs in another room. Getting sticky popcorn off their fur is not fun. And when the dog is trying to eat the popcorn off the cat's tail, things can get ugly. You've been warned.

Recipe makes approximately 20 popcorn balls.

18-20 cups popped popcorn (that's a heaping 1/4 cup of kernels)
2 cups sugar
1 cup water
1/2 cup light-colored corn syrup
1 teaspoon vinegar
1/2 teaspoon salt
1 tablespoon vanilla extract
optional extras (see below)

Preheat oven to 300 degrees F.

Remove all unpopped kernels from popped popcorn. Put popcorn in a large greased roasting pan. Keep popcorn warm in oven while making syrup.

For syrup mixture, butter the sides of a heavy 2-quart saucepan. In saucepan combine sugar, water, corn syrup, vinegar, and salt. Cook over medium-high heat until mixture boils, stirring to dissolve sugar (about 6 minutes.) Clip a candy thermometer to side of pan. Reduce heat to medium; continue boiling at a moderate, steady rate, stirring occasionally, until thermometer registers 250 degrees F, hard-ball stage (about 20 minutes.)

Remove saucepan from heat; remove thermometer. Stir in vanilla extract. Pour syrup mixture over the hot popcorn and stir gently to coat. Cool until the popcorn mixture can be handled easily. With buttered hands, quickly shape the mixture into 2-1/2" diameter balls. Wrap each popcorn ball in plastic wrap.

Note: Sometimes we colour the popcorn before forming into balls. Separate the popcorn. Add some food colour and make red and greens ones. And we've added almost every kind of candy. Chocolate chips don't work. They tend to melt. M&M's are a good and colourful way of getting chocolate into the popcorn balls. I think our favourite is candy cane pieces.

Daryl Devore lives in a century-old farmhouse in Ontario, Canada with her husband, a large saltwater aquarium, and some house ghosts. Her daughter is grown and has flown the nest. Daryl loves to take long walks up her quiet country road or snowshoe across the back acres, and in the summer kayak along the St. Lawrence River. She has touched a moon rock, a mammoth, and a meteorite. She's been deep in the ocean in a submarine, flew high over Niagara Falls in a helicopter, and used the ladies' room in a royal palace. Life's an adventure and Daryl's having fun living it.

Daryl writes erotic contemporary, historical, and fantasy romances. Her books include *A Kept Woman, Sexy Red Hood, Black Dorn*, and *Capri's Fate*. Read more about Daryl and her books at www.myeroticnotions.blogspot.com.

What's your recipe for a lasting, loving relationship?
Aretha Franklin sang it like nobody else could: R-E-S-P-E-C-T. To have a relationship last, each partner must respect the other. Respect the fact that there are going to be good days and bad days, happy moods and dark moods, major disagreements and moments of passion. Be respectful of your partner and his moods and insist on the same respect back. And on those days when you are snapping at every little thing and he complains, *nicely* (lol) point out everyone has bad days and please allow you to have yours. Instead of having a fight and creating tension between partners, respect that this is just one of those days.

Be respectful of yourself. If you don't respectful yourself, you won't be respectful to your partner. Don't belittle yourself. Because that will ooze into your daily routine and you could very possibly say something that would truly hurt your partner's feelings.

Be respectful of your relationship. Keeping a loving relationship alive takes effort. Give it the attention it needs. Smooth out the bumps, forgive the rough spots, and revel in the love. And get your Aretha Franklin groove on.

What's the best writing advice you ever received?

Send the d*#! book out. Most of us are too afraid to send our book out into the world—whether to a critique partner, a beta reader, an agent, or a publisher—because it isn't perfect. This fear comes from *your critical mind*— that voice inside your head that stops you from offering an answer or an opinion just in case it's wrong.

So now you've written a novel. You feel good about it. But to become a published author you have to *put the book out there*. And that's a terrifying experience. How do we avoid this fear? By coming up with excuses not to send our work out. This is your critical mind stifling you, stealing your creativity and peace of mind. If the book is written, send the d*#! book out.

Molly MacRae: Rhubarb Sourdough Bread Pudding

12 ounces sourdough bread ripped into 1/2"-1" pieces
1-1/2 cups milk
4 tablespoon butter
5 eggs
1-1/2 cups sugar
1/4 teaspoon salt
1 tablespoon fresh orange zest
1/4 cup crystallized ginger, chopped
4 cups rhubarb*, chopped
1/2 cup raw or brown sugar
1/4 cup pecans, chopped

Preheat oven to 350 degrees F.

*Only use the fleshy red stems. Some rhubarb is sold with the leaves still on. Rhubarb leaves are poisonous.

Spread bread on a cookie sheet and lightly toast. Place in a greased 3 qt. casserole dish.

Melt butter with milk. Pour over bread in casserole.

Mix together eggs, sugar, salt, and zest. Stir in rhubarb and ginger. Stir rhubarb and egg mixture into bread mixture. Top with sugar and pecans.

Bake for 55-60 minutes until set.

Molly MacRae writes *"murder with a dose of drollery."*—*The Boston Globe*. She's the author of the award-winning Haunted Yarn Shop Mysteries (Penguin/NAL.) Her novels include *Wilder Rumors, Lawn Order, Last Wool and Testament, Dyeing Wishes, Spinning in Her Grave,* and *Plagued by Quilt,* (a November 2014 release.) Molly's short stories have appeared in *Alfred*

Hitchcock Mystery Magazine since 1990.

After twenty years in northeast Tennessee, Molly now lives with her family in Champaign, Illinois. Read more about Molly and her books at www.mollymacrae.com.

What's your recipe for a lasting, loving relationship?
My husband and I have been married for thirty-six years, and here's our recipe: Revision is the key to success.

What's the best writing advice you ever received?
Revision is the key to success. That came from one of my high school English teachers in 1970.

Elizabeth Rose: Grilled Peaches and Vanilla Ice Cream

While growing up, I often went to visit my grandparents who lived on a Michigan lake in the middle of nowhere. And in the middle of nowhere were lots of farms, and we always had fresh fruits and vegetables right from the farmer's truck, or we picked them ourselves.

Well, one of my favorites was when we handpicked fresh peaches right off the tree in late summer. There is nothing like the taste of a fresh, juicy peach ripened by the hot summer sun.

So I'm going to tell you about a recipe I created using fresh peaches. I have to admit, I was never queen of the kitchen, but I do claim the title of queen of the grill. I even grill in the middle of a frigid Chicago winter, knee deep in snow. And while you may not have thought of grilling peaches, it is fun, easy, and delicious.

6 fresh peaches, cut in half with the pits removed
cinnamon
ground ginger
vanilla bean ice cream
sprigs of fresh mint

Sprinkle peaches with cinnamon and ground ginger. Place cut side down on a low-flame grill for about 5 minutes, until you get grill marks. Then flip the peaches, skin side down, and cook slowly until they become soft. You'll see them filling up with the peach juice like little boats.

This will take about 10 minutes. If you cook them slowly, the skins won't burn.

Serve over ice cream and top with sprigs of fresh mint. You can sprinkle with a little more cinnamon if you think you need it. Usually the peaches are sweet enough without any sweetener, but you can drizzle them with a little honey if you want. The fresh mint is a crucial part of this recipe, giving it the refreshing pop you need to finish off this succulent, creamy dessert that I call *food of the gods.*

Elizabeth Rose is the author of over thirty novels, mainly medieval, paranormal and contemporary romance. She is mostly known for her series romance which includes her Legacy of the Blade Series, Daughters of the Dagger Series, MadMan MacKeefe Series, Elemental Series, Greek Myth Fantasy Series and her small town romance series that takes place on a lake in Michigan, the Tarnished Saints Series.

She also writes short stories, and single title, which include vampire, warlock, shape-shifting and jungle romances. Elizabeth is also a freelance artist and photographer who creates all her own covers as well as her own book trailer videos. Read more about her and her books at www.elizabethrosenovels.com.

What's your recipe for a lasting, loving relationship?
Take two people who believe in romance. Add 1 heaping helping of understanding. Stir in twice the amount of communication than you think is needed. Sprinkle with a good dose of forgiveness. And top off with a good amount of unconditional love. Serve over a good helping of eating crow with a side of humble pie. Serves 2 people for the rest of their lives.

What's the best writing advice you ever received?
Don't try to make your characters do anything they don't want to do.

Characters are a lot like children. And each of my books is like birthing another child. Well, my characters tell me what to write and I more or less just take dictation. I may think I know what I want them to do or what is supposed to happen...but that's not the case. I am more surprised than anyone at what my characters say, think, or do. I just type away, and as I'm writing I am reading the story and being surprised as well. And since my characters don't want to listen to me anyway, I just let them do whatever the heck they want. It makes them more lifelike and also the main ingredients of a great story.

Helena Fairfax: Rhubarb Crumble and Custard

My mum used to grow her own rhubarb in our back garden, and one of my favourite desserts growing up was her rhubarb crumble. You can eat this dessert with cream or ice cream, but I love it most with custard. Here in the UK we often make our custard with hot milk and ready-bought custard powder, and it's delicious, but I've also given a recipe for real homemade custard, in case you prefer this or aren't able to obtain custard powder.

Preheat oven to 350 degrees F.

1 pound rhubarb*, cut into chunks
6 ounces soft brown sugar
2 ounces butter
4 ounces plain flour
2-1/2 cups milk
half a cup of single cream (not thick cream)
1 vanilla pod or half a teaspoon vanilla extract
4 egg yolks
1 ounce superfine sugar
2 level teaspoons cornstarch

*Only use the fleshy red stems. Some rhubarb is sold with the leaves still on. Rhubarb leaves are poisonous.

Place the rhubarb in a saucepan with 2 ounces of the soft brown sugar. (You can also add half a teaspoon of powdered ginger, if you like, or add a handful of chopped dried dates, which is how my mum made the dish.) Cook over a very gentle heat with the pan lid on for around fifteen minutes, stirring occasionally. After it's cooked you'll probably need to drain off some of the surplus juice.

Place the rhubarb in a pie dish.

To make the crumble topping, rub the butter into the flour until the mixture resembles bread crumbs, then stir in the remaining 4 ounces of soft brown sugar. Sprinkle the crumble mixture over the rhubarb and bake for 30-40 minutes in the centre of the oven.

To make the custard, place the milk, cream and vanilla pod in a pan and slowly bring to simmering point over a very low heat. Remove the vanilla pod.

Whisk the yolks, sugar and cornstarch very well together in a bowl with a balloon whisk. (You don't want any lumps!)

Pour the hot milk and cream onto the eggs and sugar, whisking all the time. Return to the pan, adding the vanilla extract if desired, and heat very gently, stirring all the time with a wooden spoon until the custard thickens.

Pour the custard into a jug and serve. (You can also eat custard cold, and it goes well with Jell-O. If you're leaving it to go cold, put some plastic film over the top to keep skin from forming.)

Helena Fairfax writes engaging contemporary romances with delightful heroines and heroes to swoon over. She lives in an old Victorian mill town in Yorkshire, in the north of England, near the home of the Brontë sisters. Every day Helena and her rescue dog walk the same moors beloved by Cathy and Heathcliffe, thinking up stories and plotting what happens next.

Helena's latest release is *The Antique Love*, set in an antique shop in London. A recent reader poll voted the ending "the most romantic love scene ever."

When not writing romance novels, Helena loves needlework and knitting, and once knitted an entire royal wedding...including corgis! Read more about Helena and her books at www.helenafairfax.com.

What's your recipe for a lasting, loving relationship?
A lasting, loving relationship needs both partners to show respect for each other. You must be a person that your partner can trust, and you must be able to trust your partner, in all sorts of ways. Trust each other to keep important

promises; trust each other to be reliable; trust each other to give support, and not to belittle the other one or show contempt. Mutual trust and respect are more important than physical passion for a lasting relationship...but all three together are perfect!

What's the best writing advice you ever received?

The best advice I received is never to give up. You won't get a book finished if you don't sit down to actually write it, and you won't ever be published if you give up at the first rejection. Writers need to be tenacious because writing isn't always about words flowing from the pen with the divine gift of inspiration. I wish! Writing is often a slog. Keep at it!

Lourdes Venard: Guava Rugelach

This recipe for the traditional Jewish cookie gives it a Caribbean twist with guava jam instead of the more usual apricots or raspberry. Guava jam may be hard to find in grocery stores but can be found online; Maui Upcountry Jams and Jellies makes an especially good jam. I was inspired by a book I edited, Cimarrona, *which featured made-up pastries that blended Jewish and Cuban traditional foods.*

Recipe makes approximately 40 cookies.

2 cups all-purpose flour
1/2 teaspoon salt
2 sticks (1 cup) unsalted butter, softened
8 ounces cream cheese, softened
1/2 cup plus 4 teaspoons sugar
1 teaspoon cinnamon
1 cup guava jam
1 cup loosely packed golden raisins, chopped
1-1/4 cups walnuts (1/4 pound), finely chopped
2 tablespoons milk

Whisk flour and salt in a bowl.

Beat together butter and cream cheese in a large bowl with an electric mixer until combined well. Then add flour mixture and stir with a wooden spoon. When a soft dough forms, shape it into a ball and wrap in plastic wrap. While still wrapped in plastic, flatten it into a roughly 5" x 7" rectangle. Chill until firm, 8 to 24 hours.

When ready to make the cookies, preheat oven to 350 degrees F. Line bottom of a large shallow baking pan with parchment paper.

Cut dough into four pieces. Chill three pieces, wrapped in plastic wrap. Using a well-floured rolling pin, roll remaining piece into a 8" x 12" rectangle on a well-floured surface. Transfer dough to a sheet of parchment, then transfer to a tray and chill while rolling out remaining dough in same manner, transferring each to another sheet of parchment, stacking on tray.

Whisk 1/2 cup sugar with cinnamon. Arrange one dough rectangle on work surface with long side nearest you. Using a spatula, spread 1/4 cup preserves evenly over dough. Sprinkle 1/4 cup raisins and 1/4 cup walnuts over jam, then sprinkle with 2 tablespoons cinnamon sugar.

Using parchment as an aid, roll up dough tightly into a log. Place seam side down in lined baking pan, then pinch ends closed and tuck underneath.

Make three more logs and arrange 1" apart in pan. Brush logs with milk and sprinkle each with 1 teaspoon of remaining granulated sugar.

With a large knife, make 3/4" deep cuts crosswise in dough (not all the way through) at 1" intervals. (If dough is too soft to cut, chill until firmer, 20-30 minutes.) Bake until golden, 45-50 minutes. Cool in pan on wire rack about 30 minutes, then transfer logs to a cutting board and slice cookies all the way through.

Lourdes Venard is the founder of Comma Sense Editing and a newspaper editor with more than twenty-nine years of experience writing and editing at major newspapers, including *The Miami Herald, Chicago Tribune, Milwaukee Journal Sentinel* and *Newsday*. Her freelance editing specializes in crime fiction, and several of the books she has edited have been picked up by notable small presses. She has spoken at national conferences about editing and has run training sessions for young journalists. Currently, she teaches a course for the University of California, San Diego's respected copyediting certification program. She is also editor of *First Draft*, the newsletter for the Guppies, the online chapter of Sisters in Crime. Her e-book, *A Beginner's Guide to Publishing*, will be out in October. Read more about Lourdes at www.commasense.net.

What's your recipe for a lasting, loving relationship?

Take regular walks together, or find other ways to carve out quiet time for each other. My husband and I work opposite hours, so we don't see much of each other during the workweek. Half-hour walks around the neighborhood or even to the end of our street, which opens up to a bay, afford us the time to talk about our week, and also to discuss deeper, long-term plans and dreams. We've come to some important decisions on these walks. And the bonus is that we're getting fitter at the same time!

What's the best writing advice you ever received?

I started out as a newspaper reporter, and the best advice was to write with a specific reader in mind, whether it be your mother, a friend, or a made-up reader. I find many beginning writers seem to be writing for themselves, and not for the reader. When you think outside of yourself, you will naturally craft prose that is readable and interesting.

Jessica Aspen: Dark Forest Fruit Cake

This cake is both gluten and grain-free.

4 eggs
1/2 cup pastured butter, softened
3/4 cup real maple syrup
2/3 cup canned pumpkin (or you can cook your own)
1 teaspoon vanilla extract
7 tablespoons cocoa
1/2 cup almond flour
1/2 cup coconut flour
1 cup dried cranberries or dried fruit of your choice

Preheat oven to 350 degrees F.

Mix dry ingredients, making sure to work out the lumps in the flours. Mix the wet ingredients in order. Incorporate dry ingredients into wet and blend with a mixer. Let sit for a minute so the coconut flour can absorb the moisture. Pour into greased 9" x 9" pan and bake for 30 minutes. Check for doneness with a toothpick and enjoy. This is a pretty dense cake, so watch out!

Jessica Aspen always wanted to be spirited away to a world inhabited by elves, werewolves and sexy men who walk on the dark side of the knife. Luckily, she's able to explore her fantasy side and delve into new worlds by writing spicy, paranormal romance and twisting fairy tales. She loves indulging in dark chocolate, reading eclectic novels, and dreaming of ocean vacations but instead spends most of her time writing, walking the dog, and hiking in the Colorado Rockies.

Jessica is currently working on the third book in her fantasy romance series, *Tales of the Black Court*, where three witches take on the faery queen and discover love with the fae. Read more about Jessica at www.jessicaaspen.com.

What's your recipe for a lasting, loving relationship?

Take two diverse people with nothing in common and add a large cup of physical attraction. Mix them together in a variety of life's ups and downs. Add in a spoonful of spice. And maybe one or two more for good measure. Don't forget Julia Child's advice and open a bottle of wine and pour in a little booze when it's time to celebrate. (Julia would say maybe a jot more, but it's up to you.) Shake thoroughly and bake for at least twenty years. When stored correctly will keep for another fifty.

What's the best writing advice you ever received?

The best advice I ever received was to "just write." And it's still the best advice. You can't improve or publish what isn't written, and what's the point of a book that no one reads? I know this is pretty simple, so I'll add in a few more simple pointers. Read. Read a lot. Read authors you love. Never release a book you aren't proud of. And last, but maybe most importantly: take chances. Without risk there are no books. Cheers to the risk takers!

Maegan Beaumont: Pumpkin Squares

This recipe is best if you have a cookie bar tin (looks like a cup cake tin but the wells are square instead of round.) Recipe makes approximately 2-dozen squares.

3 - 8 ounce blocks cream cheese, softened
1 cup sugar
3 eggs (2 if they're large)
1 can of pumpkin puree (15 ounces)
1-1/2 tablespoons vanilla extract
1/2 teaspoon cinnamon
3/4 cup all-purpose flour
1 pre-packaged sugar cookie mix (17.5 ounces)
2 sticks butter
4-5 cups confectioner's sugar
1/2 cup milk
cinnamon sugar (equal parts cinnamon and sugar)

Pre heat oven to 375 degrees F.

Cream 2 blocks of softened cream cheese, sugar and eggs together until fluffy. Add in pumpkin, 1 tablespoon vanilla extract and 1/2 teaspoon cinnamon, mixing together thoroughly. While mixing, add flour, a bit at a time, until fully incorporated into pumpkin mixture. Set aside.

For crust, melt 1-1/2 sticks butter. Mix into sugar cookie mix with fork until completely coated and crumbly. Set aside.

For frosting, whip remaining cream cheese and butter until completely blended. Add remaining vanilla extract. Mix. Add confectioner's sugar and milk, a little at a time, alternating between the two. The amount of confectioner's sugar and milk listed are approximations. Add both until your frosting is the desired taste and consistency.

Lightly spray tin with cooking spray. Press 2 tablespoons of crust mixture into the bottom of each well of your cookie bar tin and sprinkle generously with cinnamon sugar. Spoon 1/4 cup of filling mixture into each well, cleaning your edges as you go.

Bake for 25-30 minutes or until the tops are slightly raised and lightly golden (cracks are normal.) Remove from oven and allow to cool 10 minutes before running a butter knife around the edges of each square. Turn squares out onto a wire rack and cool before flipping over.

As soon as squares are cool, top each with frosting and sprinkle with cinnamon sugar if desired.

Maegan Beaumont is the author of *Carved in Darkness*, the first book in the award-winning Sabrina Vaughn thriller series and its sequel, *Sacrificial Muse*.

A native Phoenician, Maegan's stories are meant to make you wonder what the guy standing in front of you in the Starbucks line has locked in his basement, and feel a strong desire to sleep with the lights on. When she isn't busy fulfilling her duties as Domestic Goddess for her high school sweetheart turned husband, Joe, and their four children, she's locked in her office with her computer, her coffee pot, and her Rhodesian Ridgeback and one true love, Jade. Read more about Macgan and her books at www.maeganbeaumont.com.

What's your recipe for a lasting, loving relationship?
In one word: friendship. I met my husband when I was in high school, and long before we fell in love, we were friends. We have always been there for each other. We make each other laugh. We like each other. Our friendship has carried us through some pretty rough times and seventeen years of marriage. Love ebbs and flows but if you're lucky and smart enough to cultivate it, the friendship you build with your lover will remain constant.

What's the best writing advice you ever received?
If you ever get to a place where you think you know everything there is about writing and that your craft can't get any better than it is right now—you're wrong. At its core, writing is about exploration and expression. It never stops

moving, and it never stops growing. That means neither do you. When you start to feel complacent in your craft, it's time to shake things up!

Kay Kendall: Aunt Martha's Oatmeal Cake

Deliciously moist cake that keeps and travels well, handed down through the Texas side of my family for decades. If you can't eat nuts, then omit them and double up on the coconut for the topping. Note: This cake is easy to mix by hand. Does not require an electric mixer.

This cake is delicious immediately, but even more moist and yummy the next day. If kept tightly covered with foil or clear wrap, this cake stays moist and lovely for many days. It never lasts a week at my house, but I bet it would be good even then.

1-1/2 cups hot water
1 cup oatmeal, uncooked
1-3/4 cups brown sugar
1 cup granulated sugar
1 cup cooking oil
2 eggs
1-2/3 cups sifted flour
1 teaspoon cinnamon
1 teaspoon baking soda
dash of salt
6 tablespoons margarine or butter
2 tablespoons canned condensed milk, not sweetened
1 cup chopped pecans or walnuts (can also be toasted ahead of time before baking as a topping)
1 can Angel Flake coconut

Preheat oven to 350 degrees F.

Place oatmeal in a bowl and pour hot water over oats. Let stand while you do next steps.

Blend 1 cup brown sugar, granulated sugar, and cooking oil in a large bowl. Add eggs, sifted flour, cinnamon, soda, and dash of salt. Blend with a large spoon. Add the water-oats mixture and stir until all ingredients are well blended. Pour into greased and floured 9" x 13" pan. Bake for 35 minutes.

To make the topping, combine in a saucepan margarine, remaining brown sugar and canned condensed milk. Boil for one minute. Remove from heat. Add chopped nuts and coconut. Blend. Before cake cools, spread the topping thinly over top of cake.

Turn oven up to 500 degrees F. Return cake to oven and bake for 4-5 minutes. Watch that nothing burns since the heat is now so high. Remove from oven and cool.

Kay Kendall set her debut novel, *Desolation Row—An Austin Starr Mystery*, in 1968 in an anti-war group. The sequel is *Rainy Day Women*, set for 2015, and this time her amateur sleuth Austin Starr must convince police her best friend didn't murder women's liberation activists in Seattle and Vancouver. A fan of historical mysteries, Kay wants to do for the 1960s what novelist Jacqueline Winspear accomplishes for England in the perilous 1930s—write atmospheric mysteries that capture the spirit of the age.

Kay is also an award-winning international public relations executive who lives in Texas with her husband, three house rabbits, and spaniel Wills. Terribly allergic to the bunnies, she loves them anyway! Her book titles show she's a Bob Dylan buff too. Read more about Kay and her books at www.kaykendallauthor.com.

What's your recipe for a lasting, loving relationship?
Four ingredients make for a lasting, loving relationship. Here are the four C's:
* Caring
* Commitment
* Communication
* Conflict resolution.

If your relationship has those elements, then chances are yours will go the distance. If things feel rocky, then analyze against those four C's. Get yourself to a trained therapist if you are having trouble with conflict resolution, which of course rests on being able to communicate well. Many couples have the first two—caring and commitment—but founder on the next two. Luckily, with help and persistence, communication and conflict resolution can be learned. And just because you and your partner talk all the time does not mean that you are actually *communicating*. That's a tricky one.

What's the best writing advice you ever received?

Be persistent and never give up. Most authors I know make some false starts before they publish their first novels. It may take a decade to accomplish your goal, but if you burn to write, then do keep at it. The manuscript for my first novel I cannibalized for my second, so all that work was not wasted. And my second manuscript became a published book last year. One male mystery author says that *writing is like an informal game of golf—you get all the mulligans you want.* While you are practicing, take time to learn the craft. The Internet provides a wealth of information.

Take writing classes. Attend book signings. Find a mentor. Participate in a writing group, as I have for many years, but finding the right fit for yourself is key. Constructive criticism should be the rule, and if the group or even one member delights in tearing people down, then run for the hills. Writers' psyches are fragile, and you want to be around supportive folks. Also, attend writing conferences. You can learn from them, but they're also networking opportunities. All writers should network—publishing is a relentless business.

Elizabeth John: Apple Cake

1-1/2 cups sifted flour
2 teaspoons baking powder
1/2 teaspoon salt
1/2 cup sugar
1 teaspoon cinnamon
1/2 cup unsalted butter
3 tablespoons unsalted butter, melted
1 egg
1/2 cup milk
2 cups baking apples, peeled and sliced

Preheat oven to 400 degrees F.

Sift together flour, baking powder, salt and 1/4 cup sugar in a large bowl. Cut in butter with a pastry blender until mixture resembles coarse pebbles.

Beat egg in a small bowl. Add milk to egg and blend together.
Add milk/egg mixture to dry ingredients. Stir enough to blend.

Spread dough in lightly grease 9" x 9" x 2" pan. Place sliced apples on top of dough. Mix together 1/4 cup sugar and cinnamon. Sprinkle over apples. Drizzle melted butter over the top. Bake 30-35 minutes or until cake tester comes out clean.

Elizabeth John developed a love of reading and writing in early childhood, which continues to this day. She's published many newspaper and magazine articles and several short stories. For a few years, she enjoyed writing ceremonial resolutions for her state's senators and assembly members. When she's not penning contemporary romances and romantic suspense novels, she's teaching elementary school children how to read and write.

Elizabeth's debut novel, *Judging Joey,* soon to be released by Soul Mate

Publishing, is a sweet, contemporary romance with a touch of intrigue. Admittedly, she's a TV and movie junkie and has noble intentions to practice yoga daily. Her day job, family, and writing life keep her busy. In her spare time, she can be found walking her dogs, sharing a meal with friends, gardening, or relaxing at the beach with her nose in a good book. Read more about Elizabeth and her writing at www.elizabethjohn.com.

What's your recipe for a lasting, loving relationship?
Ah, one of the mysteries of life. My husband and I married in our early twenties and have been together thirty years. Okay, so now you can figure out how old I am. Let me just say that no relationship is perfect, but I think to be successful, it has to have key elements. Our relationship is based on trust. Without it, we wouldn't be together. For me, it's non-negotiable. No matter what life swings my way, I choose to be happy and care about my spouse's happiness. There will be times when tragedy strikes, making this most challenging.

Aside from those moments, how do I create happiness? I try to include laughter in my daily life. Couples who laugh and have fun reduce stress. We find activities to do separately and together. My husband hikes, and I read. He likes war movies, and I like comedies, but we walk the beach together, swim in the pool, and enjoy museums and the theater. I have lots of friends, but he's my best friend, which leads me to the essentials of tolerance and acceptance.

In the end, does it really matter if one person leaves dishes in the sink and the other eats the last of the ice cream? Everyone is unique and you're never going to "change" someone else. Knowing that enables us to tolerate our differences and accept one another's "faults."

The most important ingredient in a loving and lasting relationship recipe is forgiveness. When you're with someone a long time, chances are they will do something that will need to be forgiven. I suggest taking a deep breath and think ahead five years. Will whatever happened be detrimental to your relationship's future? If not, let it go, and your relationship will continue to grow and fulfill you.

What's the best writing advice you ever received?

The best advice is from Nora Roberts. She says writers have to put their butt in the chair and write, and she can always fix a page she's written, but not a blank one. Talking about writing, thinking about it, telling people you're a writer doesn't make it true. The act of writing makes it true. The more you write, the better your writing. That's why so many writers admit to having manuscripts "under their bed" that will never see the light of day and never be published. It's because writing is an art, and artists create through practicing their craft.

Lots of things can get in a writer's way. Day jobs, family commitments, chores, social media, the business side of writing, the list goes on. There will always be something to compete with your writing time. Don't let it. Prioritize and balance things in your life.

Many writers advise letting dust bunnies grow and leaving beds unmade because writing is more important. Well, I tried to ignore the laundry piling up and the breakfast crumbs on the counters, but I found it actually hurt my creativeness. For me, clutter causes chaos, and I can't write around chaos. So here's another great writing tip from Susan Meier. It's called *The 10-Minute Solution*. Decide on something you'd like to get done (and it can be writing) and set a timer for ten minutes. Everyone can find ten minutes during the day. Those clothes in the laundry basket can get folded. In fact, when I set the timer, I find I move faster to see how much more I can do. It becomes a cardio workout for me, too! And I don't feel the least bit guilty when I sit my butt back in the chair to write.

Victoria Adams: Anita's Tarts

This is a four-generation family Christmas tradition. Anita was my grandmother's close friend.

2 eggs
3/4 cup brown sugar
1/2 cup corn syrup
1/2 cup coconut
6 tablespoons margarine
3/4 cup nuts (chopped pecans or walnuts)
1 tablespoon vinegar
pinch salt
small patty shells, at least 18 (You can make your own or buy frozen ones.)

Preheat oven to 425 degrees F.

Mix ingredients together stirring thoroughly. Arrange patty shells on a cookie sheet. Fill each with a tablespoon of mixture. When you fill the shells, stir constantly as the nuts and coconut drop down in the liquid. The liquid boils while baking and fills in the patty.

Bake for about 15 minutes on middle rack in the oven. Watch carefully the first couple times you make them so you can judge the heat and time needed in your oven.

Victoria Adams has been writing since she was little. Being an only child, long car rides were filled with making up stories in her head about the people she saw out the car window. When her daughter was younger, she made up stories that her daughter suggested. She'd say, "Once upon a time there was a...." and her daughter would shout, "Chicken!" The story would progress from there.

This turned out to be a great creativity exercise for her future life writing contemporary romance, New Adult romance, and flash fiction. Her books include the Circles Trilogy (*Dancing in Circles, Circles Divided,* and *Circles*

Interlocked) and *A Guy and A Girl.*

Victoria lives in Ontario, Canada with her husband and pets. She likes to garden, cook, and study Raqs Sharqi (Egyptian belly dance.) Read more about Victoria at www.victoriaadams.blogspot.com.

What's your recipe for a lasting, loving relationship?

This September, my husband and I will be celebrating our thirty-second wedding anniversary. On our wedding day—let me repeat that—*on* our wedding day—several people told my husband that the marriage would never last. So how did we manage to prove them all wrong? Two words—love and humour. (I'm Canadian, remember. We throw the letter U all over the place.)

Love. (noun) a profoundly tender, passionate affection for another person.

How wonderful it is that the definition doesn't include terms like *always, all the time,* and *every waking moment of every day.* Do I feel a profoundly tender, passionate affection for my husband *all* the time? No. There have been times—numerous times—when I wanted to stick a stamp on his forehead and mail him to Bora Bora. With no return address! Then there are those times when I feel loved from my nose to my toes, snuggling up next to him on the couch watching a Star Trek episode for the hundreth time.

Humour (noun) a comic, absurd, or incongruous quality causing amusement.

There isn't one specific moment in our marriage that I can jot down that will make you laugh, but our days are often filled with laughter. It's our sharp wits and enjoyment of life that keep us happy and laughing. That laughter is never at the expense of the other. We aren't caustic or sarcastic. We are playful and teasing. After thirty-one years, we know each other pretty well and we know the lines not to cross.

So my advice for a lasting, loving relationship: remember to love and laugh. Happy loving people—happy loving relationship.

What's the best writing advice you ever received?

I don't know that I was ever given any writing advice, but I was inspired by the following quote: *"If you can tell stories, create characters, devise incidents, and have sincerity and passion, it doesn't matter a damn how you write."* – W. Somerset Maugham (British novelist – 1874-1965)

Many years ago, I wrote with total abandon. It was a joy. Stories flowed out of my fingertips. Then the work began. I had to learn *how to write*, which made no sense because I knew how to do it. But what I didn't know were the *rules* of writing. Trying to fit my stories within the confines of those rules was a soul-crushing experience, and it drove me away from my laptop. When I read my edited stories, my voice was gone. I thought if that was how I was supposed to sound then I couldn't write, and I wouldn't write.

Then I bumped into Maugham's quote and a ray of sunshine filled my heart. Okay, a bit overly dramatic, but it was a writing-life changing moment.

Since then I have developed my own personal philosophy of my writing style—Picasso wasn't always Picasso. He used to be just a guy called Pablo who painted strange pictures.

No, I'm not saying I'm as good at writing as Picasso was at art. I'm saying he stepped out of the box and did it his way, which is what I do. Yes, it's scary out here. Many writers vehemently disagree with me. I often get scolded. Yes, there are moments when I feel I'm wrong. At those times, my spirit shatters. But I go back to Maugham's quote, regain my confidence, take a deep breath, and keep on writing. Because I am me, and that is who I write like.

C.L. Pauwels: Great-aunt Zella Kirkendall's Friendship Cookies

1 cup Crisco shortening
1-1/2 cups granulated sugar
1 cup brown sugar
2 eggs, slightly beaten
1 cup undiluted canned milk
1 teaspoon baking soda
1 tablespoon white vinegar
1 teaspoon vanilla extract
4 cups flour
2 teaspoons baking powder
1/2 teaspoon salt
1/2 cup confectioner's sugar

Preheat oven to 350 degrees F.

In a large bowl cream shortening, one cup of granulated and the brown sugar. Add eggs. Mix well.

In a large measuring cup combine the canned milk, baking soda, vinegar and vanilla extract.

Combine flour, baking powder, and salt.

Add milk mixture and dry ingredients to sugar mix, alternating one-half of each at a time, ending with milk mixture.

Combine remaining granulated sugar and powder sugar.

Drop one teaspoon of dough at a time into sugar mixture and roll gently to coat. Bake on ungreased cookie sheets 10-12 minutes until just set and lightly brown on the bottom. Do not over-bake! Store tightly covered.

For a holiday variation, add red or green decorating sugar to coating mix.

C.L. (Cyndi) Pauwels writes mystery and crime novels. *Forty & Out*, her debut novel, was released through Deadly Writes Publishing in September 2014. Her short fiction has appeared in *Mock Turtle* 'zine, *Over My Dead Body!*, *The View from Here* (UK), and other journals. In 2009, she published a non-fiction book, *Historic Warren County: An Illustrated History*, and Sugati Publications has selected two of her essays for their *Reflections from Women* anthology series.

In addition to writing, Cyndi's portfolio career includes book editing (*The Enduring Legacy of Kahlil Gibran* and *The Essential Rihani*), teaching freshman composition as an adjunct at a local community college, and serving as assistant director for the Antioch Writers' Workshop.

Cyndi lives in Yellow Springs, Ohio with her husband of thirty-six years, George, and three spoiled dogs. They have two grown children and one grandson. Read more about Cyndi and her writing at www.clpauwels.com.

What's your recipe for a lasting, loving relationship?
Communication. Commitment. Respect. Realistic expectations. I just read a student's final paper where she took a (humorous?) look at the dating scene, and her goals and expectations made me cringe. Granted, my husband and I have been together since high school, so I've never faced the (apparent) nightmare that is dating in today's world. From what our children and friends have gone through—and still experience—that's probably a good thing. I'd likely still be single.

But how do those ingredients break down?

Communication: If I need something, I need to say so (same for Hubby). As much as we'd like to believe otherwise, neither of us is a mind reader.

Commitment: My parents divorced when I was very young, and between them they have been married nine times. How am I still on number one?

Because I made a commitment to work at my marriage, and I reaffirm that commitment every day. Maybe not consciously, but the intent is there. Only abuse or Hubby's desire to leave would end our life together.

Respect: For him, for myself (that's the tough part!) and for us.

Realistic expectations: Hollywood and fairy tales and romance novels are not reality. There are days I don't like Hubby very much (and vice versa, I'm sure!) but I always love him (see: Commitment).

Has it been easy? Good heavens, no. But few worthwhile things are. We work at our relationship together—separate individuals, but stronger as a team. And I wouldn't have it any other way. He's my best friend. When we have a problem, we deal with it together, not on Facebook or Twitter or with a pal. Our relationship has evolved considerably since high school, but it's never been better than it is today.

What's the best writing advice you ever received?
The value of writing advice tends to vary depending on the stages of my career, and I would imagine "When the student is ready, the teacher appears" applies to writing as much as it does to other areas of life. In the early days when I focused on journalism, it was a Dragnet-like "Just the facts." And there's always the old saw of "Write what you know."

In 2005, during my first stab at National Novel Writing Month, founder Chris Baty encouraged us to turn off the internal editor and just get the words on the page—an important step for anyone attempting a novel! (Hallie Ephron's version is, *"Hold your nose and write!"*)

At the Antioch Writers' Workshop (AWW) in 2009, lecturer Zakes Mda turned conventional wisdom upside down and urged us to write what we *don't* know—explore new worlds, new ways of being, and infuse them with the emotions and reactions of our life as we do know it.

In 2010, as I was finishing my first complete novel as my master's thesis, my advisor struggled to convince me there's a big difference between thesis-ready and publication-ready. She was so right! I'm not sure that book will ever see the light of day, but I learned a great deal in the process of writing it.

During this year's AWW, Andre Dubus III instructed us to be "authentically curious," yet "willing to fail" as we write.

The take-away from all those years? Listen to the advice of so-called experts, but be true to myself, and to my story. Keep reading, keep learning. But above all, keep writing.

Alice Loweecey: Grandma's Cheesecake

2 cups graham cracker crumbs
1/2 cup powdered sugar
1/2 cup melted butter
1 pound ricotta
1 pound cream cheese
1 cup sugar
4 eggs (at room temperature)
1 teaspoon vanilla extract
juice of 1/2 fresh lemon
3 tablespoons flour
3 tablespoons cornstarch
1 stick melted butter (not margarine)
1 pint sour cream

Preheat oven to 320 degrees F.

Combine first three ingredients. Press firmly onto bottom of 9" spring-form pan.

Cream ricotta and cream cheese in large bowl. Add sugar gradually. Continue beating until smooth. Add eggs and stir until smooth. Stir in lemon juice and vanilla extract. Add flour and cornstarch, then add melted butter and beat until smooth. Blend in sour cream and beat until smooth. Pour into spring-form pan.

Bake one hour, then turn off oven and allow cake to remain in oven two hours longer. DO NOT OPEN OVEN! Refrigerate.

Alice Loweecey, baker of brownies and tormenter of characters, recently celebrated her thirtieth year outside the convent. She grew up watching Hammer horror films and Scooby-Doo mysteries, which explains a whole lot. Her current books are *Force of Habit*, *Back in the Habit*, and *Veiled Threat*.

Her newest in the series, *Nun Too Soon*, arrives in January 2015. When she's not creating trouble for her sleuth Giulia Falcone, she can be found growing her own vegetables (in summer) and cooking with them (the rest of the year.) Read more about Alice and her books at www.aliceloweecey.com.

What's your recipe for a lasting, loving relationship?

My recipe for a lasting, loving relationship is to mix patience with thoughtfulness, toss in a generous handful of humor, a sprinkling of playfulness, and season with lots of hugs, kisses, and time together. Add in sex as desired (no pun intended!) and remember silence can be as companionable as conversation.

What's the best writing advice you ever received?

The best writing advice I ever received was from an agent who made me think outside of the writing cage I'd created for myself. I'd labeled myself a horror writer, and he suggested I try mystery. I didn't ignore the suggestion and opened up a whole new field of ideas to turn into books. Labels are for canned food. We can write whatever we want!

June Shaw: Grandma's Bread Pudding

10 slices bread

2 cups milk

8 ounce can evaporated milk

1 cup sugar plus 3 tablespoons

1 teaspoon vanilla extract

1/4 cup butter, melted

4 eggs separated

3 tablespoons sugar

4 egg whites

Preheat oven to 450 degrees F.

Pour milk and evaporated milk into a bowl. Break the bread into pieces and soak a few minutes in the milk. Add egg yolks, 1 cup sugar, melted butter, and vanilla extract. Using your hands, mix well.

Pour mixture into a greased 8" x 10" x 2" pan. Bake for 15 minutes.

For the meringue, place egg whites in a mixing bowl and beat until firm. Gradually add 3 tablespoons sugar and beat until stiff peaks form. Pour meringue over the bread pudding and bake an additional 3-5 minutes until meringue turns golden brown.

June Shaw was a Deadly Ink Best Mystery of the Year nominee for *Relative Danger*, the first book in her Cealie Gunther humorous mystery series featuring a spunky widow trying to avoid her hunky ex-lover on her quest to rediscover herself. Unfortunately, he opens Cajun restaurants wherever she travels, and she can't avoid both tempting dishes and men. *Killer Cousins* and *Deadly Reunion* continue the series.

June's suspense novel, *Approaching Menace*, has been compared to works by Mary Higgins Clark. Often readers say her *Nora 102 ½: A Lesson on Aging*

Well is the most inspirational book they've read in a long time.

June serves on the board of Mystery Writers of America's Southwest Chapter and is the Published Author Liaison for the South Louisiana chapter of Romance Writers of America. Read more about June and her books at www.juneshaw.com.

What's your recipe for a lasting, loving relationship?
Show your partner love. Express it, too. My husband died when we had five young children. Sometime later I met my squeeze, Bob. He'd been married, too, and had seven children. We started dating and have kept it up for decades. He lives a few blocks from me and comes over a few hours every evening unless we're going out or on a trip. "Why don't y'all get married?" lots of people have asked us, to which we reply, "This works. Why change it?"

Both having a number of grandchildren, Bob and I touch each other every day. A gentle tap on the shoulder. A little kiss on the head (the top of his is bald.) We give each other hugs and tell each other, "I love you" many times a day. We hold hands during parts of a mass. Intimacy comes in many forms. Showing and expressing your love, I believe, is the best.

What's the best writing advice you ever received?
Don't give up. I decided I wanted to be a writer when I was in ninth grade, but we didn't have creative writing classes, and I stayed busy with extra-curricular activities and a boyfriend after that. I married right out of high school and during the next six years, gave birth to five children. Sometimes I would think about writing, but life stayed so busy that I seldom found time to read, much less try writing a book.

After my husband died, I finished college and started teaching English to junior high students. With all of their papers to grade and my own children's events to attend, few creative words would come. I did manage to experience the excitement of selling a few essays to periodicals.

I had begun teaching late, so after twenty years I could retire. My sweet children were blessing me with grandchildren. Then I sold a novel. My family cheered. After the first book, I sold more and kept going.

The person who had told me that if I wanted to be writer, I should never give up, offered terrific advice, which I found holds true for almost every area of life. I believe that my family and I are enjoying my writing success so much because it took so long for me to reach this point. My advice to everyone: If you want something really badly, don't give up if you can't reach your dream right away. Maybe, like me, you'll get to bask in your achievement and enjoy it even more later.

Donnell Ann Bell: Toasted Strawberry Shortcake

In fiction calories never count.

1/4 cup Grand Marnier plus 1 tablespoon
1 loaf pound cake
3 cups sliced strawberries
2 tablespoons sugar
1/2 pint whipping cream

Cut pound cake into 1" slices. Brush with Grand Marnier and broil until toasted on both sides.

Slice strawberries, toss with sugar. Let stand at room temperature.

Whip cream with 1 tablespoon Grand Marnier.

Place 1 slice toasted pound cake on plate. Top with strawberries and whipped cream.

Donnell Ann Bell grew up in the Southwest and today calls Colorado home. A homebody at heart, she leaves the international thrillers to world travelers and concentrates on suspense that might happen in her neck of the woods— writing *suspense too close to home.* She's the author of the e-book bestsellers *The Past Came Hunting, Deadly Recall,* and *Betrayed.* Her fourth book, *Buried Agendas,* is due out in the fall of 2014.

Donnell's books have won or been nominated for prestigious writing awards, including The Epic Award for Best Thriller Suspense, Greater Detroit's Booksellers Best for Best First Book and Best Single Title, and the Daphne du Maurier Award for Excellence in Mystery Suspense. She's also the co-owner of Crimescenewriters, a Yahoo group for mystery/suspense writers. Read more about Donnell and her books at www.donnellannbell.com.

What's your recipe for a lasting, loving relationship?

A sense of humor and to be in a relationship with your best friend. Without those two ingredients, it's like trying to bake a cake at high altitude without additional flour.

What's the best writing advice you ever received?

First, don't fall in love with your own words. Words are tools. Second, finish the book. Even if you've been writing for years on proposal, there's something masterful and rewarding about working through from beginning to middle to end. And finally, find your own voice.

T. Michelle Nelson: Tiramisu Cupcakes

This recipe will make approximately 20 cupcakes.

1-1/4 cups cake flour (not self-rising,) sifted
3/4 teaspoon baking powder
1/2 teaspoon sea salt
1/4 cup milk
1 vanilla bean, halved lengthwise, seeds scraped and reserved
4 tablespoons unsalted butter, at room temperature, cut into pieces
3 whole eggs plus 3 egg yolks, at room temperature
1-1/4 cups granulated sugar
1/3 cup plus 1 tablespoon freshly brewed very strong coffee (I set my Keurig
on the small setting and used Dark Magic)
1 ounce Marsala (or sweet red wine)
1 cup heavy cream
8 ounces mascarpone cheese, room temperature
1/2 cup confectioner's sugar, sifted
unsweetened cocoa powder

Preheat oven to 325 degrees F.

Sift together cake flour, baking powder, and salt.

Heat milk and vanilla bean pod and seeds in a small saucepan over medium
heat just until bubbles appear around the edge. Remove from heat. Whisk in
butter until melted. Let stand 15 minutes. Strain milk mixture through a fine
sieve into a bowl, and discard vanilla bean pod.

With an electric mixer on medium speed, whisk together whole eggs, yolks,
and 1 cup sugar. Set mixing bowl over a pan of simmering water, and whisk by
hand until sugar is dissolved and mixture is warm, about 6 minutes. Remove
bowl from heat. With an electric mixer on high speed, whisk until mixture is
fluffy, pale yellow, and thick enough to hold a ribbon on the surface for several
seconds when whisk is lifted.

Gently but thoroughly fold flour mixture into the egg mixture in three batches. Stir 1/2 cup batter into the strained milk mixture to thicken, then fold milk mixture into the remaining batter until just combined.

Line muffin pans with paper liners. Divide batter evenly among lined cups, filling each 3/4 full. Bake, rotating tins halfway through, until centers are completely set and edges are light golden brown, about 20 minutes. Transfer tins to wire racks to cool completely before removing cupcakes.

To make the syrup, stir together coffee, wine, and 1/4 cup sugar until sugar is dissolved. Let cool.

Brush tops of cupcakes evenly with coffee-wine syrup. Repeat until all syrup has been used. Allow cupcakes to absorb liquid 30 minutes. (Don't skimp or they won't have that tiramisu taste; it just ends up tasting like pancakes.)

With an electric mixer on medium speed, whisk heavy cream until stiff peaks form (Be careful not to overbeat, or cream will be grainy.) In another bowl, whisk together mascarpone and confectioner's sugar until smooth. Gently fold whipped cream into mascarpone mixture until completely incorporated.

Dollop frosting immediately onto cupcakes. Refrigerate up to overnight in airtight containers. Dust generously with cocoa powder just before serving.

T. Michelle Nelson is an American author of paranormal romance. Her titles include *Life and Death of Lily Drake, 'Til Death Do Us Part, Death Warmed Over, The First Time,* and *Sick to Death.* She became enamored with vampires at an early age when she watched George Hamilton in *Love at First Bite.* As she got older, her tastes leaned more toward the dark and morose, but her love of all things vampire never wavered.

T. holds a degree in Elementary Education from Murray State University. Her first book was released by Inkspell Publishing in 2012. When she isn't writing, T. enjoys traveling, eating ridiculously carb-laden foods, music and canoeing. She will be working on a new series once the conclusion of the Lily Drake series releases in June of 2014 but looks forward to enjoying some down time with her son, family, friends, and her little dog. Read more about T. and her books at www.tmichellenelson.com.

What's your recipe for a lasting, loving relationship?

The person you choose to spend your life with should be a partner. Relationships are going to have hard times. Work through them and know it's okay to fight; just don't stay mad.

What's the best writing advice you ever received?

Grow a thick skin. Not everyone will gush over you and love your writing. Not everyone should.

Nina Milton: Bara Brith

I live in Wales where bread is 'bara' and dried fruit is 'brith' (pronounced breeth.) You can buy several varieties of Bara Brith fruit bread, but this is my own celebratory recipe, which won first price at the local Garden Produce Show.

10 ounces mixed dried fruit (a mix of lots of sultanas and raisins and some currants)
12 ounces warmed 'brew' (a mix of hot black tea with brandy)
3 ounces light soft brown sugar
1 large egg
grated rind and zest of one lemon
12 ounces self-rising whole-meal flour
1 teaspoon mixed spices
tiny pinch of salt
2 ounces granulated sugar (golden is better than white)
2 ounces water

Preheat oven to 350 degrees F. (after soaking is complete)

Soak the fruit in the tea and brandy mixture overnight.

The next morning, drain the fruit, reserving the liquid. Place fruit in large mixing bowl. Stir in flour, lemon zest, spice, salt and sugar. Add the egg and about half the reserved liquid. Mix well, adding more of the liquid until you have a soft dropping consistency. If it's a little stiff, add more brandy or black tea.

Transfer the mix to a 1-pound loaf tin and bake for approximately 40-45 minutes. It should have risen and be firm to the touch. A toothpick might not come out perfectly clean because of the moisture in the fruit, but if you think it needs longer and is getting too brown on top, cover with foil and reduced the heat slightly. When fully baked, turn out the bara onto a cooling rack.

Make a sugar syrup by gently heating the granulated sugar in the water until dissolved then boiling vigorously for about 1 minute. Allow to cool then pour over the top of the bara. Once the syrup has set, you can slice the cake and enjoy, but this bara is even better the following day (and for several days,) especially when spread with butter.

Nina Milton writes both children's books and crime fiction. She began her writing career by publishing short stories in magazines and anthologies and won several writing competitions. *In the Moors* and *Unraveled Visions* are the first two books in her Shaman Mystery series, featuring shaman Sabbie Dare. Her books for children include *Sweet & Sour* (HarperCollins) and *Tough Luck* (Thornberry Publishing.)

In 2004 she gained an MA in Creative Writing and since then has tutored and run creative writing workshops. She also writes course materials for the Open College of the Arts. Read more about Nina and her books at www.kitchentablewriters.blogspot.com.

What's your recipe for a lasting, loving relationship?
My recipe for a lasting, loving relationship is to keep falling in love with each other over the years.

What's the best writing advice you ever received?
The best writing advice I've ever received is get yourself a writing buddy—someone who understands about writing and can offer good, impartial advice...and can happily share a commiserating drink or a celebratory glass of champagne!

P.A. De Voe: Fudge Brownies with Spelt Flour

While the ancient spelt grain is in the wheat family, spelt flour has more protein than wheat flours (17% versus 13.7% in whole grain wheat.) For you history buffs, it was an important grain in Europe from the Bronze Age into Medieval times.

2 - 1 ounce squares unsweetened chocolate
1/3 cup butter
3/4 cup spelt flour
1/2 teaspoon baking powder
slightly less than 1/2 teaspoon salt
1 cup sugar (or 3/4 cup of agave)
2 large eggs
2 teaspoons vanilla (made with vodka)
slightly more than 1/2 cup broken walnuts

Preheat oven to 350 degrees F.

Melt chocolate and butter together, cool to lukewarm.

Mix flour, baking powder, and salt together in bowl.

Using a stand mixer, beat sugar and eggs together on medium speed. Combine the chocolate-butter mixture, vanilla, and egg-sugar mixture. With mixer on low speed, gradually add flour mixture. Stir in walnuts, blending well.

Spread evenly in lightly greased 7-1/2" x 11" pan. Bake on center rack for 25 minutes or until toothpick comes out clean.
Cool on wire rack.

If desired, top with chocolate frosting.

P.A. (Pam) De Voe, a cultural anthropologist, has worked with American Indians, Asians, American expatriates, and refugees and immigrants. Her strong interest in our traditions, including the stories we tell to pass on our values and history, provides a springboard for her characters and stories.

A Tangled Yarn, Pam's first published mystery, debuted in 2013 as part of Annie's Publishing's Mystery-a-Month Book Club. Since then, Pam has been immersed in Ming Dynasty China. In 2014 she had two short stories of her magistrate Judge Lu's case files ("Legacy: A Father's Day Mystery" and "Judge Lu's Dilemma") published in the *Fish or Cut Bait* anthology.

Currently, Pam is also working on her Mei-hua young adult, historical adventure/mystery trilogy set in 1380 and scheduled to debut in 2015. Read more about Pam and her writing at www.padevoe.com.

What's your recipe for a lasting, loving relationship?

First: *respect.* The person you will spend so much time with and will share your life decisions with must be someone you respect. But what does respect mean? Respect means different things to different people. For some, it means a clear demarcation of roles. For others, it means sharing in everything and in every decision. In either case, respect is how you value and support your partner's abilities, dreams, and goals, as well as his or her personal time and space. This is the foundation of love.

Second: *trust.* Trust is so necessary because as you are building a family, you can't possibly still put your partner in the number one position he or she enjoyed before children came into your lives. In my opinion, once children are part of the family and are growing, they are the family's top priority. So, you will find you actually neglect your partner in many everyday situations, maybe for long periods of time (depending on the needs of your particular offspring), but you must still be able to trust your partner will be there—supportive, loyal, and, yes, loving. This situation may take years of your married life! There will be respites, periods when you can bask in each other's love, but really, these periods will be brief.

What's the reward? The reward is an envelope of *love,* not only in the family you've created, but also in your personal one-on-one relationship. This evolving love will have certainly mellowed and grown beyond your initial expectations. For who in the throes of youthful passion understands the fullness of a love that's withstood both irritating small assaults and enormous crises over the years? That's love.

What's the best writing advice you ever received?

This is difficult because there is so much to learn and every piece of information, whether initially seemingly large or small, can have such a great impact on your writing.

I think for me it's advice I received but misunderstood: "Find your voice." I thought this meant find P.A. De Voe's voice. But that's not it. "Find your voice" really means to find the right voice to engage the reader in the story *you* want to create.

In other words, if I want to write a cozy mystery, such as *A Tangled Yarn*, I need to develop a voice reflecting small town sensibilities and a craft-oriented and mutually supportive network of friends who are faced with the problem of finding a murderer to keep justice from going awry.

However, when I write my Chinese Ming Dynasty Mei-hua series or my Judge Lu short stories, I must find and use the best voice that both mirrors the historic period and engages my contemporary reader. In other words, I am definitely not looking for *my* voice. I am looking for the voice that best conveys the most interesting and exciting story to the reader—while being true to historic details and context.

In the end, this is the challenge of being an author. Much like an actor, we become different personas as we write within our genre or sub-genre.

Skye Taylor: Apple Chocolate Chip Cake

2 cups flour

1 teaspoon cinnamon

pinch salt

1 teaspoon baking soda

1 cup sugar

3/4 cup oil

2 eggs

2 teaspoons vanilla extract

1/2 cup chocolate chips

3 cups sliced apples

Preheat oven to 350 degrees F.

Sift dry ingredients. Mix in eggs, oil, vanilla extract, and chocolate bits. Add flour mixture and mix well. Fold in apples. Pour into greased and floured tube/bundt pan.

Bake for 1 hour.

Skye Taylor, a native New Englander, is now a transplanted Yankee soaking up the sun, warmth, and history of St. Augustine, Florida. She's a mom and grandmother who retired early to spend her days writing, walking the beach with her four-footed sidekick MacDuff, and trying to keep her to-be-read pile from taking over the house. She believes life is an adventure, so when her kids were grown, she joined the Peace Corps and lived in the South Pacific for two years. She's jumped out of perfectly good airplanes and earned a basic sky diving license, and she loves to travel.

Her published novels to date include *Whatever It Takes*, *Falling for Zoe*, and *Loving Meg*. She's a member of Romance Writers of America, Ancient City Romance Authors, and Florida Writers Association. Read more about Skye and her books at www.skye-writer.com.

What's your recipe for a lasting, loving relationship?
I believe that the most durable and loving relationships begin with friendship. Truly "liking" each other, admiring and celebrating who each really is, rather than entering a relationship blinded by love or lust and believing you can change the things you don't like.

Although all good romances in fiction end with a happy ever after, usually at the altar or headed there, a lasting, loving relationship is not a fairy tale following a declaration of love. Good relationships require work. They require faithfulness, patience, acceptance, humor and the ability to forgive, because no one is perfect and we all make mistakes.

Also important: as the saying goes, don't judge a book by its cover. Some of the handsomest men are mean, demanding and self-centered, and some of the prettiest women are vain, petty and manipulative. It's the person inside the package that counts. Fall in love with your best friend's heart and soul and mind, then give unstintingly of your own heart, soul and mind.

Lasting, loving relationships require two generous, loving hearts and are blessed with the unshakable belief that this is the person you were meant to be with forever, through all the ups and downs life has to throw at you, through the good and the bad, the happy and the sad, and everything in between.

What's the best writing advice you ever received?
There are so many pieces of good writing advice I've received, it's hard to pick out just one. I'd have to say "write what you know" is a good place to start, but let's face it, time travel, while intriguing, is not really possible. And historical fiction requires a ton of research to fill in what you don't know. Unless you plan to write a long series with one or two main characters, then research will be required to vary the careers and personalities. So once again, research is a must.

Be a people-watcher. Pay attention to how people act, think, speak, move. The opportunities are endless—in waiting rooms, at the grocery store, the airport, your child's school, parties, the beach, the opera—everywhere there are people.

Writers also need to grow a thick skin. This is because to become a really good writer, you must become vulnerable. You have to put your work out there where it will be critiqued and reviewed. Learn how to accept criticism, then go back and make your writing better.

Lastly, LOVE WHAT YOU DO. Write because you can't imagine a life that doesn't include writing. Write because there are people and stories in your head begging to be put into words. Write because you love doing it.

Conda V. Douglas: Soda Cracker Pie

This recipe was handed down from my grandmother to my mother to me. My grandmother was the first to make this, and she made it often during the Great Depression, when making a dessert could be a challenge, as ingredients were often too expensive. But soda crackers were always cheap and available, and it only takes a cup of sugar for an entire pie. The pie is a touch salty, but that makes it all the tastier. This recipe is also the first dessert I did all by myself at the age of only nine. It's that simple.

3 egg whites

1/2 teaspoon cream of tartar (any more and the pie will be chewy)

2 teaspoons vanilla extract

16 saltine crackers

1 cup sugar

1 cup pecans or walnuts or raw or toasted—not salted—peanuts

(Loosely medium chopped nuts work best. Other nuts don't work well. You can omit the nuts, but pie will be very plain and very dense)

1 teaspoon cinnamon (optional)

1/2 teaspoon nutmeg (optional)

whipped cream topping (Real whipped cream topping made by hand from heavy cream is best on this pie, and this is the only way my grandmother would top it. I confess I occasionally use vanilla ice cream. FYI, any other flavor of ice cream tends to obscure the taste of the pie.)

Note: If you wish to make the pie taste like "apple pie," add a teaspoon of cinnamon and optional 1/2 teaspoon of nutmeg.

Preheat oven to 325 degrees F.

Beat eggs whites until quite stiff. Add cream of tartar.

Crush crackers into medium to fine crumbs (not fine as flour.) I like to do this the old fashioned way: put the crackers in a gallon sized Ziploc plastic bag and use your fists to beat the crackers. It's fun!

Gently fold crackers, vanilla extract, sugar and nuts into egg whites.

Pour into a well-greased pie plate and bake 25-30 minutes. Pie will be a light brown and crusty.

Cool pie completely. Add whipped cream right before serving.

Conda V. Douglas grew up in the ski resort of Sun Valley, Idaho. Her childhood brimmed with authors, artists and other creative types, plus goats in the kitchen, buffalo bones in the living room, and rocks in the bathtub. Now her life is filled with her cat, her dog, her permanent boyfriend, and writing.

She's traveled the world from Singapore to Russia and her own tiny office, writing all the while. She delights in writing her *Starke Dead* mystery series, featuring jeweler Dora Starke. The more Dora discovers cursed jewelry, her aunt digging graves, and a rampant poisoner, the more fun Conda has—although sometimes Dora complains about her plight! Next up, *Starke Raving Dead*, in which Dora's mad Aunt Maddie proves the aptness of her name. Read more about Conda www.condascreativecenter.blogspot.com.

What's your recipe for a lasting, loving relationship?
Start with a wonderful base of mutual respect and interest. Add several brimming cups of listening to your beloved, and leaven with a strong sense of your own individuality. Bake and watch your love rise and increase. Delightful and delicious!

What's the best writing advice you ever received?
Joseph Campbell's *"Follow your bliss."* My bliss is writing and so I've worked hard to do just that, and sometimes, when writing, have succeeded.

Pepper Phillips: White Chocolate Bread Pudding

This recipe serves 6-12.

16 ounce loaf King's Hawaiian Bread
3 whole eggs
7 egg yokes
4 cups heavy whipping cream
1 cup milk
1/2 cup sugar
1/2 teaspoon salt
1 teaspoon vanilla extract
24 ounces white chocolate (I used Hershey's Premium White Chips)

Preheat oven to 350 degrees F.

Cut bread into 1" squares and place in very large bowl.

Whisk eggs and egg yolks until blended.

Pour 3 cups cream, milk, sugar, salt and vanilla extract into saucepan and heat, but don't bring to boil. When milk/cream mixture is hot, add 12 ounces white chocolate and stir until chocolate is melted. Remove from stove. Slowly pour into the eggs, stirring constantly. Slow is the key. Then pour over the bread and mix until bread soaks in the mixture.

Spray a 9" x 13" baking pan with cooking spray. Pour bread into baking dish. Cover with foil. Bake 30 minutes. Remove foil and bake an additional 10 minutes.

To make sauce, heat 1 cup heavy whipping cream and 12 ounces white chocolate chips in saucepan over medium heat, stirring until chips melt. Pour over individual servings of bread.

Pepper Phillips wrote her first play in the seventh grade. But before that she read every book in her age group at the small local library in Northeast, Maryland. An only child for years, she entertained herself in the worlds she created in her mind. She's still pretty mindless in some respects, but her writing world is where she is the happiest. Her novels include *The Devil Has Dimples*, *Naomi's Heart*, *The Vow*, *Unconditionally*, and *The Christmas Gift*. Read more about Pepper and her books at www.pepperphillips.com.

What's your recipe for a lasting, loving relationship?
I've been married for fifty-two years. You have to treat your spouse with love, respect and courtesy. He needs to be your best friend. Treat him like you'd like to be treated. It works for us.

What's the best writing advice you ever received?
Read. Read. Read. Write. Write every day. Finish what you write.

Judy Alter: Mary Helen's Mother's Coffee Cake

Mary Helen was a girl in TCU pre-school with Colin, my oldest child, way back when in the '70s. For a parents' potluck, we were all assigned recipes, and I was given this one. I didn't know about taking the cake out after five minutes, so I let it sit and cool. When I did take it out, half the cake came out, and the other half stayed in the pan. After that, Mary Helen's father always called me the "two-cake lady," because I had to bake it again and do it right. But it is an absolute favorite of all my children when done with chocolate cake mix and chocolate pudding. But you can experiment with flavors. I had a friend who made it with strawberry, which didn't sound very good, but vanilla or lemon would work. We just happen to be chocoholics.

1 box cake mix
1 box instant pudding
1/2 cup oil
4 eggs
1-1/2 cups sour cream
sugar and cinnamon

Preheat oven to 350 degrees F.

Mix together everything but sugar and cinnamon. Spray bundt pan with Pam or similar coating. Mix cinnamon and sugar and sprinkle on all sides of prepared pan. Add the batter, evening it out as much as possible (it's a thick batter,) and top with more cinnamon and sugar.

Bake for 50-60 minutes or until a long kebab skewer or piece of dry spaghetti inserted in center comes out clean. The cake often has to cook longer. Cool five minutes, then remove from the pan. DON'T WAIT LONGER THAN FIVE MINUTES.

Judy Alter, an award-winning novelist, is the author of five books in the Kelly O'Connell Mysteries series: *Skeleton in a Dead Space, No Neighborhood for Old Women, Trouble in a Big Box, Danger Comes Home,* and *Deception in*

Strange Places. She also writes the Blue Plate Café Mysteries—*Murder at the Blue Plate Café* and *Murder at the Tremont House.* Coming in October 2015 is *The Perfect Coed,* perhaps the start of a new series.

Her work has been recognized with awards from the Western Writers of America, the Texas Institute of Letters, and the National Cowboy Museum and Hall of Fame. She has been honored with the Owen Wister Award for Lifetime Achievement by WWA and inducted into the Texas Literary Hall of Fame.

Judy is retired as director of TCU Press and the mother of four grown children and the grandmother of seven. She and her Bordoodle Sophie live in Fort Worth, Texas. Read more about Judy and her books at www.judyalter.com.

What's your recipe for a lasting, loving relationship?

I've been single for thirty years, which tells you my recipe for a good marriage didn't work. But I have wonderful children, and we had great years together as they were growing up. Today, we are all close and can't wait for the next time we can be together.

Here's my recipe for a happy family:
Start with a lot of love. Mix in some firm rules, respect, a willingness to share, and a willingness to listen. Season with lots of laughter, more than a few pets, a lot of "extended family," and frequent meals together. Grows better the longer it simmers. Stir and mix frequently.

What's the best writing advice you ever received?

The best writing advice I ever received came from the prolific and successful mystery writer, Susan Wittig Albert. She was signing books at a TCU event one day when I was bold enough to tell her about my ambition to write mysteries. She immediately asked if I belonged to Sisters in Crime, and when I said, "No," she replied, "Join."

I did, became active in the Guppies chapter, and began to learn about the world of mysteries, which is a far different world from that of fiction about the American West and its women. In six or eight years, I have learned more than I ever imagined, and I am beyond grateful for the support and comradeship.

The next best writing advice came years ago when I wrote a scholarly 60-page pamphlet for the Boise State Western Writers Series. It bounced right back with the first ten pages heavily edited for things like passive voice, tense change, pronoun switches, etc. I learned a lot from editing the rest of the manuscript, following the example of the editor's work. I'm happy to say the pamphlet was published.

Cadence Denton: Becky's Hummingbird Cake

2 cups cake flour
2 cups granulated sugar
1 teaspoon salt
1 teaspoon baking soda
1 teaspoon cinnamon
3 eggs, beaten
1-1/4 cups vegetable oil
2-1/2 teaspoons vanilla extract
2 cups bananas, mashed
1 cup apples, chopped (we prefer Granny Smith)
8 ounces chunk pineapple, drained
2 cups pecans, chopped
8 ounces cream cheese, room temperature
16 ounces confectioner's sugar
1 stick butter, room temperature
1 cup sweetened flaked coconut

Preheat oven to 350 degrees F.

Combine cake flour, granulated sugar, salt, baking soda, and cinnamon in a large mixing bowl. Add egg and oil, stirring (by hand) until dry ingredients are moistened. Stir in 1-1/2 teaspoons vanilla extract, 1 cup pecans, bananas, pineapple, and apple. Stir well. Pour into a greased bundt pan and bake for 70 minutes. Cool in pan for 10-15 minutes. Remove cake from pan and cool on baking rack.

To make frosting, in a medium mixing bowl, beat butter and cream cheese until smooth. Add remaining vanilla extract. Blend. Gradually add confectioner's sugar. Spread on cool cake. Gently pat coconut on outer ring of cake and sprinkle remaining pecans on the top.

Cadence Denton makes her home in a sleepy little Louisiana town on the banks of the Mississippi River. She began her journey to publication when her daughter retorted, "Writing is your dream, not mine." And so it was. And so it remains.

Cadence writes dark paranormal romance, light paranormal romance, time travel, light science fiction, and horror. She is the stay-at-home mother of five, four dachshunds, and one perpetually confused cocker spaniel.

She presently has two series, The Immortal Firewalkers, a dark paranormal romance and Wicked Palate, a kinder, gentler paranormal romance series based on a Cooking Network whose star chefs are all supernaturals. Learn more about Cadence and her books at www.cadencedenton.com.

What's your recipe for a lasting, loving relationship?

I would have to say mutual respect and friendship are key. Looks fade, hormones come and go, but having a partner you respect as an equal in the relationship is indispensable. And really, isn't mutual respect the bedrock for all friendships? There are days when you might not be feeling the romance; those are the times you really need your mate to be a friend. Friends have each other's backs. Friends are with you through thick and thin.

What's the best writing advice you ever received?

I've been blessed with tons of great advice, and heaven knows I need every scrap of advice. However, I'd have to say the one bit of advice that has helped me the most is the bit that sounds so simple, and yet is so hard to achieve: Keep writing.

That's it. Sounds easy, right? For me, writing is a love-hate, dysfunctional-family-on-the-Jerry-Springer-show relationship. I love, love, love writing when the writing fairy has come for a visit and the words are flowing through my fingers like a great, black river. Hours later, the river of ink has dried up and the word drought is making me want to pull my hair out. Every single word comes at a snail's pace. That's when I'm ready to say to hell with this and pull out the chalk paint. But I don't. I keep writing.

Lesley A. Diehl: Butternut Valley Ginger Stout Cake or Muffins

A Recipe for Those Who Hate Beer. Don't drink the beer; eat it instead! With the recent popularity of craft beers, more individuals are trying beers locally brewed and finding them right tasty. As with wine, those who love to cook are looking for ways to incorporate beer into their dishes. Usually, we think about beer and the savory, but this recipe is for a sweet dish—muffins or cake. Stout is one of those beers that works well in both types of dishes, but is particularly suited for these spicy muffins. And it pairs well with chocolate, intensifying the taste of the chocolate, much like adding coffee to a chocolate cake. If you like these muffins, you might want to try making a stout float with either vanilla or chocolate ice cream. Delicious!

2 cups all-purpose flour

2 teaspoons ground ginger

1-1/2 teaspoons baking powder

1-1/2 teaspoons baking soda

3/4 teaspoon ground cinnamon

1/2 teaspoon salt

1/4 teaspoon ground cloves

1/2 cup (1 stick) butter, softened

1 tablespoon candied ginger (finely chopped) or 1 teaspoon ground ginger or 1 tablespoon grated fresh ginger

1 cup granulated sugar

1/2 cup packed light brown sugar

3 large eggs

12 ounces stout (Use your favorite stout from a local microbrewery. I do!)

1/2 cup molasses

Preheat oven to 350 degrees F.

Combine flour, ground ginger, baking powder, baking soda, cinnamon, salt, and cloves. Set aside.

Beat butter and candied ginger with electric mixer on medium speed until combined. Add sugars, beating to combine. Add eggs, one at a time, beating well after each addition.

Mix stout and molasses together. Add to wet ingredients. Alternately add dry ingredients in three additions, with the beer mixture, beating until combined and scraping down side of bowl as needed. Batter will be runny.

Pour batter into greased muffin pans or 9" x 13" baking pan. (do not overfill, especially if making mini-muffins). Bake 12-18 minutes. Makes over 24 regular muffins or around 80 minis. If using a 9" x 13" baking pan, bake 45 minutes. In both cases, muffins or cake is done when toothpick inserted into the center comes out clean.

Note: Cake and muffins do not round up when baked.

Try with a dollop of ginger spiced whipped cream or top with a slice of crystallized ginger or both.

Lesley A. Diehl retired from her life as a professor of psychology and reclaimed her country roots by moving to a small cottage in the Butternut River Valley in upstate New York. In the winter she migrates to old Florida— cowboys, scrub palmetto, and open fields of grazing cattle, a place where spurs still jingle in the post office, and gators make golf a contact sport. Back north, the shy ghost inhabiting her cottage serves as her writing muse. When not writing, she gardens, cooks and renovates the 1874 cottage with the help of her husband, two cats, and, of course, Fred the ghost, who gives artistic direction to their work.

Lesley is the author of several mystery series and a number of short stories. All her work features country gals with attitude. Read more about Lesley and her books at www.lesleyadiehl.com.

What's your recipe for a lasting, loving relationship?
It took me over fifty years to find my partner-for-life. I think I'm a slow learner when it comes to establishing a love relationship. But it was worth the

wait. Here are some of the ingredients I've found necessary for an enduring relationship:

The main ingredient for lasting love sounds simple but takes commitment. Never assume what you have is what you will always have. Relating is something you redo every day and sometimes in different ways.

The yeast you use to get the relationship to live for the duration is found in shared core values. Know your values, and if you choose someone who shares them, half your work is done. There are plenty of other things to argue about. You don't need to fight about moral stances on issues.

Here's the spicy part: When you discover how imperfect your partner is, understand he or she is finding out the same about you. Tolerance goes a long way toward making the relationship work.

As with any recipe, some days it turns out better than others. There will be times when the relationship seems to have gone off its wheels. Hang in there. If you healed before, you can heal again.

People are like fine wine and aged cheese. Being old has its advantages. I'm clearer now about what I believe, but I'm also more forgiving. Thank goodness we're aging together.

There's always a pinch of something that makes your love special. For me, it's a sense of humor. It doesn't hurt if your partner has one, too. Laughter is like a really good butter crème frosting. It makes the sweet treat you call your relationship even sweeter.

What's the best writing advice you ever received?
You write, so be proud to call yourself a writer. It only feels odd the first time you say it, and then it's who you are.
Join professional writers' organization such as Sisters in Crime, Guppies and Mystery Writers of America to connect with other writers. You'll find their help and advice invaluable.

Write every day. Make writing a priority.

Finally, be generous. Help other writers become the best they can be.

Erin Farwell: Hidden Treasure Cookies

This recipe will make 4-dozen cookies and can be made with three different fillings.

1/3 cup Crisco
1/3 cup sugar
1 egg
1/4 cup milk
1-1/2 teaspoons baking powder
2 cups flour
1/2 teaspoon salt
1 teaspoon vanilla extract
fluffy vanilla frosting

Preheat oven to 375 degrees F.

Beat shortening, sugar, and egg until light and well blended. Mix in remaining ingredients.

Roll out dough. Cut with 2-1/2" to 3" round cookie cutters. Place dough circles in small muffin tins. Add chocolate, caramel, or date filling (see below.) Bake for 12 to 15 minutes or until light brown. Place on rack to cool. Frost when completely cooled.

Chocolate Filling:
12 ounces semi-sweet Baker's Chocolate coarsely chopped
2/3 cup evaporated milk

Cook in pan over low heat until thick and smooth.

Caramel Filling:
70-75 caramels (approximately 21 ounces)
2/3 cup evaporated milk
Cook in pan over low heat until thick and smooth.

Date Filling:
1 pound dates, chopped
1/2 cup sugar
1 cup water

Cook until thick and smooth. (I've never made these, but if you like dates I'm told they are excellent.)

Note: May use microwave to make fillings instead of stovetop, if desired.

Erin Farwell has degrees in business and law but currently writes fiction and teaches art classes. Her novel, *Shadowlands*, is set in 1927 Chicago and her short story, "The Carver" is published in the *All Hallow's Evil* anthology. She is also a freelance writer, specializing in business documents, articles, blogs, editing, and ghostwriting. As an artist, she works with Metal Clay, a clay-like material that has pure silver, copper, and bronze in it. It can be molded and shaped like clay but when fired in a kiln, the clay is burned away, leaving pure metal behind. Read more about Erin and her books at www.erinfarwell.com.

What's your recipe for a lasting, loving relationship?
Listen more than you speak, and evaluate any action you take from the perspective of those you love.

What's the best writing advice you ever received?
Eliminate as many distractions as possible, and don't let research become a way to avoid writing.

Regan Walker: Blueberry Kuchen

This is a great summer recipe. Half the blueberries are cooked, half raw. It's light and refreshing and low in calories (if you can resist serving it without vanilla ice cream!) It's one of my favorites!

1-1/2 cups plus 2 tablespoons flour
1/8 teaspoon salt
1/2 cup plus 3 tablespoons sugar
3/4 cup (1-1/2 sticks) butter, slightly softened and cut into small pieces
1-1/2 tablespoons white vinegar (I use white peach vinegar)
6 cups fresh blueberries
1/8 teaspoon cinnamon

Preheat oven to 400°F.

In medium bowl, mix 1-1/2 cups flour, salt and 3 tablespoons sugar. Cut in butter until it resembles coarse crumbs. Sprinkle with vinegar and shape into dough. At this point, I recommend chilling the dough for a half hour as it's very sticky otherwise, but you can skip this.

With lightly floured fingers, press dough into pan (I use a larger pottery dish for this, but you can use a 9" spring-form pan, in which case you'll use less of the dough and only 5 cups blueberries.) Spread the dough about 1/4" thick on bottom, less thick and 1/2" high around sides (1" if using a spring-form pan.)

Mix 3 cups of the blueberries with remaining 2 tablespoons flour, 1/2-cup sugar and cinnamon. Spoon the mixture on top of the dough.

Bake on the middle rack for 35-45 minutes or until crust is golden brown and the filling bubbles. Remove from oven and place on a cooling rack. Top with remaining 3 cups raw blueberries. (They kind of mush together, which is just what you want.)

Cool for at least 30 minutes. Run a paring knife around the crust edge to separate from the pan before opening spring-form. In my pottery dish, I've never had any trouble getting it to come out in neat slices.

Regan Walker loved to write stories as a child, but by the time she got to college, more serious pursuits were encouraged, so she became a lawyer. But after years of serving clients in private practice and several stints in high levels of government, she decided it was time for a change. She returned to her first love of writing. Her work had given her a love of international travel and a feel for the demands of the "Crown," so her first novels, the Agents of the Crown trilogy, involve a demanding prince who thinks of his subjects as his private talent pool.

In 2014 Regan ventured into the medieval world with *The Red Wolf's Prize*, a William the Conqueror romance. Regan wants her readers to experience history and adventure as well as love. Each of her stories weaves in history and real historical figures.

Regan lives in San Diego with her Golden Retriever who reminds her every day to smell the roses. Read more abut Regan and her books at www.reganwalkerauthor.com.

What's your recipe for a lasting, loving relationship?
I daresay I have learned what I'm about to tell you through failure, rather than success, but I'm pretty confident it works.

To begin with, there has to be a lifelong commitment. You will not always feel the early pangs of being "in love." There will be days, possibly even years, when you will be distracted by work or kids and even angry at your spouse. Especially for women, it's important to know he is there for life. No outs. And build in the recognition that forgiveness is necessary.

There has to be chemistry, of course. I am always amazed when I listen to a man in his fifties or sixties describe his wife. I'm fairly certain he still sees her as the younger woman he married. In his mind, she is still attractive long after her fur has worn off (to quote *The Velveteen Rabbit*.) Marry for love. If you can't live without him (or think you can't,) he might be the right one.

Opposites may attract, but the more you have in common the easier it will be. One of my past relationships was so easy it was often like being with myself. He and I were different, of course. He did a lot of eye-rolling "guy" things. But at heart, we shared the same values, a commitment to faith and family, and we both loved to read and discuss ideas. Try to find someone who likes to do what you do, who is like you at your core. Then you'll enjoy each other for life!

What's the best writing advice you ever received?
Write what you love to read, finish the book, get a good editor, and keep striving to improve.

Kaye Spencer: Poor Man's Cake *c.* 1930

1 cup raisins
1 cup water plus 1 tablespoon
1/2 cup shortening
1 cup sugar
1 egg, beaten
1 teaspoon baking soda
1/2 teaspoon salt
1/2 teaspoon ground cinnamon
1/2 teaspoon ground cloves
2 cups flour
1 cup confectioner's sugar
1/4 teaspoon vanilla extract

Preheat oven to 350 degrees F.

In medium sized saucepan, boil raisins in 1 cup water until about 1/2 cup of water remains and raisins have plumped. Set pan with raisins and water aside to cool.

When cool, add sugar, egg, baking soda, salt, cinnamon, and cloves. Mix well. Add flour and mix until batter is smooth.

Spread batter evenly over lightly greased jellyroll pan. Bake 15 minutes. Cake is done when nicely browned, edges pull away from sides, and center is springy to touch.

For frosting, mix together confectioner's sugar, vanilla extract, and 1 tablespoon water. Frosting should be smooth, thin, and drizzly. Add more water if necessary. While cake is still hot, pour frosting over top. After cooling, store lightly covered to prevent cake from drying out.

Kaye Spencer, a native Coloradoan, creates romances from her basement hovel in a quiet little neighborhood on the southeastern plains. While all genres are within her story-crafting realm, she is drawn to the Old West—truths, myths, and legends alike. Growing up on a ranch, listening to Marty Robbins' gunfighter ballads, watching the "classic" television westerns, and reading Louis L'Amour westerns all contributed to her lifelong interest in the Old West.

In addition to writing, Kaye edits romance book reviews for Joyfully Reviewed. Retired from a long career in education, Kaye is enjoying the life of a fulltime writer and avid spoiler of grandchildren. A history nerd, Kaye regularly Tweets history trivia. Read more about Kaye and her books at www.kayespencer.wordpress.com.

What's your recipe for a lasting, loving relationship?
There's nothing that can't be solved with a good laugh, a long talk, and a bottle of wine. Love—no matter how it ends—is about the ride. Ultimately, it's about the sharing and the memories.

What's the best writing advice you ever received?
I have three bits of writing advice that sum up everything I need to keep me on the path to productive writing.

There's a word for a writer who never gives up...published. – J.A. Konrath

Write when you can. Finish what you start. Edit what you finish. Submit what you've edited. Repeat. – J.A. Konrath

Writing is rewriting. A writer must learn to deepen characters, trim writing, intensify scenes. To fall in love with a first draft to the point where one cannot change it is to greatly enhance the prospects of never publishing. – Richard North Patterson

Barbara Monajem: Victorian Currant Bread

I love trying out old recipes. I adapted this one from "A Nice Plum Cake" in Beeton's Book of Household Management, *which was published in 1861. Mrs. Beeton's recipe doesn't contain plums and neither does mine, so I'm calling it currant bread instead.*

3 cups flour
3 teaspoons baking powder
1/2 teaspoon soda
1/2 teaspoon salt
1 cup brown sugar
1 stick butter, softened
1-1/4 cups milk
1-1/2 cups currants
1/3 cup diced candied lemon peel (optional)

Preheat oven to 350 degrees F.

Mix the flour, baking powder, soda and salt together. In a large bowl, cream the butter and sugar. Add the dry ingredients alternately with the milk and mix well. Add the currants and lemon peel and stir until thoroughly mixed.

Fill a greased loaf pan about 2/3 full and bake for 45-50 minutes or until a toothpick comes out more or less clean.

Old-fashioned cookbooks don't give specific information about pan sizes. This recipe made too much batter for my loaf pan, so I made the remainder into muffins. They were great, too. In fact, if you prefer, you can just make muffins instead. The only difference is that the cooking time is shorter, about 20–25 minutes, depending on the size of the muffin pans.

Barbara Monajem grew up in western Canada. She wrote her first story, a fantasy about apple tree gnomes, when she was eight years old, and dabbled in neighborhood musicals at the age of ten. At twelve, she spent a year in Oxford,

England, soaking up culture and history, grubbing around at an archaeological dig, and spending her pocket money on adventure novels. Thanks to her mother, she became addicted to Regency romances as well. Back in Canada, she wrote dreadful teen melodramas and studied English literature. She spent several years in Montreal and published a middle-grade fantasy when her children were young. Now her kids are grown, and she has written a number of award-winning books for adults, including several Regency novellas and the Bayou Gavotte series of contemporary paranormal romances.

Barbara now lives in Georgia, USA, with an ever-shifting population of relatives, friends, and feline strays. Read more about Barbara and her books at www.BarbaraMonajem.com.

What's your recipe for a lasting, loving relationship?

Have good intentions, and assume your partner has good intentions, too. That way you won't be quick to misjudge, and you'll nourish love instead of hurt feelings. You'll always be willing to talk things through and try to understand one another better.

What's the best writing advice you ever received?

I've received so much good advice that it's very hard to choose...but the piece of writing advice I refer to most often is, "Be hard on your characters." I'm soft-hearted by nature, so it's quite a stretch for me to make things difficult for my characters—but difficulties and the process of overcoming them are what make for a good story.

Kathleen Kaska: Bananas Kaska

Bananas Foster was created in 1951 by Paul Blangé at Brennan's Restaurant in New Orleans. Whether prepared tableside at a romantic restaurant by a copacetic sous-chef, or simply made at home for a quiet dinner, this dessert speaks intimacy. It's something to be shared, a dish to rekindle the spark of romance. Here's my version:

1/4 cup unsalted butter
1/2 cup dark brown sugar, packed
4 tablespoons Christian Brothers Brandy
2 ripe bananas, halved, each half sliced lengthwise
1/4 teaspoon ground cinnamon
1/4 teaspoon ground nutmeg
2 scoops maple ice cream

Melt butter in a medium skillet over low heat. Add brown sugar, cinnamon and nutmeg. Stir with a wooden spoon until sugar dissolves. Add bananas and cook until caramelized on both sides (about a minute per side.) Spoon sauce over bananas while cooking.

Remove bananas from pan and place in a separate dish. Bring sauce to barely a simmer and add brandy quickly. *Immediately but carefully ignite sauce with a long-stick match or long-stem lighter. Cook until the flame dies, and the sauce turns into a slightly thick syrup (about two minutes.)

Return the bananas to the pan and coat with sauce. Divide mixture into two serving dishes. Top each with a scoop of ice cream. Serve while sauce is still warm.

*Caution: Pre-measure brandy—don't guess. Flame might rise above pan. Stand back when igniting.

Kathleen Kaska grew up "a good girl" in West, Texas during the 1950s. She began writing her 50's era Sydney Lockhart Mystery series (*Murder at the*

Arlington, Murder at the Luther, Murder at the Galvez, and *Murder at the Driskill*) to say and do things she would have "never tried at home."

Kathleen also writes the Classic Triviography Mystery Series (*The Agatha Christie Triviography and Quiz Book, The Alfred Hitchcock Triviography and Quiz Book*, and *The Sherlock Holmes Triviography and Quiz Book.*) Her Alfred Hitchcock and Sherlock Holmes trivia books were EPIC award finalists in non-fiction.

When not writing, Kathleen spends much of her time with her "pilot," traveling the country's back roads and byways, bird-watching, and looking for new locales for her mysteries. Her passion for birds led her to write *The Man Who Saved the Whooping Crane: The Robert Porter Allen Story* (University Press.) Read more about Kathleen and her books at www.kathleenkaska.com.

What's your recipe for a lasting, loving relationship?
2 parts early romantic experiences, rekindled
2 parts new ones, well planned
4 parts respect
4 parts patience
7 parts prayer

Mix well. Serves two.

What's the best writing advice you ever received?
While attending a writing conference early in my writing career, I had a five-minute pitch session with an editor. Being nervous and inexperienced in this sort of thing, my well-rehearsed spiel lasted about thirty seconds. I filled a couple of more minutes by telling him my lofty promotional plans for the book. Then I asked him what he thought. Smiling he replied, "Okay, but *finish your book.*"

What he was telling me was to stay focused—promotion means nothing if you don't have a book to sell. And that my first draft would probably not be a literary masterpiece, but with a finished product, I'd at least have something tangible to mold into a final manuscript that could catch the attention of an agent or editor.

I never forgot those three words of wisdom. And my pilot always reminds me, in everything, to touch first-base first. I'm still writing. I also lead writing workshops for novices. They all get the same advice at the end: *finish your book*.

Catherine Kean: Chocolate Chip Coconut Cheesecake Bars

1-1/2 cups graham cracker crumbs
1/3 cup sugar plus 2 tablespoons
1/3 cup butter, melted
8 ounce package cream cheese
1 egg
1 teaspoon vanilla extract
1 tablespoon grated orange peel
1 cup chopped walnuts or pecans
1 cup semisweet chocolate pieces
2/3 cup flaked coconut

Preheat oven to 350 degrees F.

In a large bowl, combine graham cracker crumbs, 2 tablespoons sugar, and melted butter. Press into an ungreased 9" x 13" pan. Bake for 7-8 minutes.

In a medium bowl, beat cream cheese, 1/3 cup sugar, egg, vanilla extract, and orange peel until well blended. Spread evenly over crust.

In a small bowl, combine nuts, chocolate pieces, and coconut. Sprinkle evenly over cream cheese mixture, pressing in lightly.

Bake 25-28 minutes or until golden brown. Cool in pan. Cut into squares. Store in refrigerator.

Catherine Kean is an award-winning author whose love of history began with visits to England during summer vacations. Her British father took her to crumbling medieval castles, museums filled with artifacts, and historic churches. Her love of the awe-inspiring past stuck with her as she completed a B.A.(Double Major; First Class) in English and History. After finishing a Post Graduate course with Sotheby's auctioneers in England, she worked in

Canada as an antiques and fine art appraiser.

Catherine wrote her first medieval romance while her baby daughter was napping. Her books were originally published in paperback and have been translated into several foreign languages. Her stories have won numerous accolades, including the Gayle Wilson Award of Excellence. Her novels also finaled in the Next Generation Indie Book Awards and the National Readers' Choice Awards.

Her books include: *Bound by His Kiss* (Novella,) *Dance of Desire, My Lady's Treasure*; her Knight's Series (*A Knight's Vengeance, A Knight's Reward, A Knight's Temptation*, and *A Knight's Persuasion*); and several boxed sets (*Medieval Rogues, Magnificent Medieval Men, Magnificent Medieval Champions, Daring Damsels*, and *Knights of Valor*)

Catherine lives in Florida with her husband, daughter, and two spoiled cats. Read more about Catherine and her books at www.catherinekean.com.

What's your recipe for a lasting, loving relationship?
Trust, honesty, respect, and unconditional love.

What's the best writing advice you ever received?
Get the rough draft of your story done. Once the "skeleton" is there, go back and rework, refine, and polish, but don't worry initially about fixing scenes and tweaking dialogue until the draft is finished. It's amazing what you will discover about your characters, plot, and story theme in the first writing that you might not have known early on.

Rose Anderson: To Die For Crème de la Crème

Food is such a sensual thing. It nourishes the body and mind in so many ways. The first time I tasted this heavenly dessert it was presented with little creamy hearts floating on a sea of mashed raspberries. It came to me at a staff party at the school where I once worked. Begging the recipe from the office manager/chef, I made it myself. Because it's wonderful and highly addictive, I've only made this dessert a few times. I hope you try it at least once. I know you'll lick the beaters. I think I had my face in the bowl!

Disclaimer: This is so good you'll have a hard time deciding if you should eat it or rub it all over your body. I take no responsibility for stains the latter incurs.

1/2 cup farmer's cheese
1/2 cup crème fraiche or sour cream
1-1/4 cups sugar
2 teaspoons fresh lemon juice
2/3 cup heavy cream, very cold
4 pints raspberries, rinsed and drained (Any fruit would be good, berries, peaches etc.)

Combine farmer's cheese, crème fraiche (or sour cream,) 1/4 cup sugar, and 1 teaspoon lemon juice until well blended. Whisk in heavy cream and whip until your mixture has the texture of whipped cream. This will happen fairly quickly. As soon as it looks like thick whipped cream stop or you'll get lumpy butter chunks in sweet whey.

Refrigerate. If you'd like a prettier presentation, this mixture molds really well but be sure to line molds with cheesecloth. If you chill this a little first, you can plop it onto waxed paper and roll it into a log. Then chill and slice when firm. While that's firming up, prepare the topping.

Mash raspberries and mix with remaining sugar and lemon juice.

Unmold, spoon, or slice your crème mixture into serving dishes. Top with raspberries.

Rose Anderson is multi-published, award-winning author and dilettante who loves great conversation and discovering interesting things to weave into stories. She lives with her family and small menagerie amid oak groves and prairie in the rolling glacial hills of the upper Midwest. Her active imagination compels her to write everything from children's stories to historical non-fiction. Read more about Rose at www.calliopeswritingtablet.com.

What's your recipe for a lasting, loving relationship?
I was fortunate to have found my soul mate early on. We've been together nearly forty years. I'd say the key to a lasting, loving relationship is sharing laughter. Life has highs and lows. Finding humor in the lows and laughter in the highs makes living and loving fun.

What's the best writing advice you ever received?
Write for yourself.

Lynn Cahoon: Pumpkin Marble Cheesecake

16 ounces cream cheese (2 packages)
3/4 cup sugar
1 teaspoon vanilla extract
3 eggs
1 cup pumpkin
3/4 teaspoon cinnamon
1/4 teaspoon nutmeg
graham cracker crust (pre-made)
whipped cream

Pre-heat oven to 350 degrees F.

In a large bowl, cream together cream cheese, sugar, and vanilla extract. Mix in eggs one at a time, beating after each. When smooth, set aside 1 cup of the mixture in a separate bowl.

Fold in pumpkin, cinnamon, and nutmeg to the larger quantity of batter. Pour into a graham cracker crust. Pour the one cup of batter you set aside in four separate dollops onto the pie. Run a knife through the dollops to gently marble the mixture into the pumpkin.

Bake for 55 minutes. Cool. Serve with lots of whipped cream.

Lynn Cahoon is a *USA Today* and *New York Times* bestselling author. If you visited the Idaho town where she grew up, you'd understand why her mysteries and romance novels focus around the depth and experience of small town life. She currently lives with her husband and four fur babies in a small historic town on the banks of the Mississippi River where her imagination tends to wander.

Lynn's books include The Tourist Trap Mysteries (*Guidebook to Murder*, *Mission to Murder*, and the November 2014 release, *If the Shoe Kills*;) her Bull

Rider series (*The Bull Rider's Brother*, *The Bull Rider's Manager*, and *The Bull Rider's Keeper*;) and the paranormal Council series (*A Member of the Council* and *Return of the Fae*.) Read more about Lynn and her books at www.lynncahoon.wordpress.com.

What's your recipe for a lasting, loving relationship?

Flexibility. (Now stop laughing.) I didn't mean in the bedroom, although, sometimes that's a good thing, too. I believe for a relationship to work you have to be willing to give 100 percent at times, and get 100 percent at times. It's a give and take. Sometimes I'm too focused, thinking there's only one way to get something done. My way. I've learned to step back and at least consider another way. If you can see the other person's side, you can at least pinpoint what's the problem rather than reacting emotionally.

What's the best writing advice you ever received?

Finish the darn book. Seriously, there's no reason to be talking about the business or career of writing without doing the work. Finish the book, and let it simmer. Then send it off into the world, and start another one. Write, submit, repeat. Your craft will improve, and you'll have a ton of inventory once the publishing world discovers your genius. Besides, you may not know what book you're writing until it's done.

Suzie Tullett: Melt in the Middle Chocolate Puddings

This recipe takes only fifteen minutes to prepare and another fifteen minutes to cook. Serves 8.

10 ounces dark chocolate
4 tablespoons butter
5 eggs
1/2 cup sugar
3/4 cup all-purpose flour
1-1/2 teaspoons baking powder
pinch of salt

Preheat oven to 325° F.

Melt chocolate and butter in a large bowl over a saucepan of simmering water. Remove from heat.

In another large bowl, beat the eggs and sugar until light and fluffy. Add the flour, baking powder, salt, and melted chocolate. Mix with a spoon until well blended.

Divide the mixture evenly into 8 lightly greased ramekins. Bake for about 15 minutes until the cakes have just cooked through. The cakes should still look a bit moist on top. Remove from oven and allow to cool for 5 minutes.

Suzie Tullett is an author of contemporary, humorous fiction and romantic comedy. Her novels include *Going Underground* and *Little White Lies and Butterflies*, which was short-listed for The Guardian's 2013 Not the Booker Prize. She has a Master's Degree in Television & Radio Scriptwriting and worked as a scriptwriter before becoming a fulltime novelist. Read more about Suzie and her books at www.suzietullett.com.

What's your recipe for a lasting, loving relationship?
When it comes to creating that lasting, loving relationship, recipes can vary

according to taste. For me, though, there are a few key ingredients. Without sounding corny, ingredients like mutual respect, understanding and appreciation. And because, as with most things in life, there are bound to be hiccups along the way, I like to introduce a lot of laughter and a degree of tolerance into the cooking process.

For me, however, the one thing that binds all these ingredients together is honesty.

It's natural to bicker over who keeps leaving the toothpaste cap off the tube or why the dishwasher hasn't been emptied *again*. At times, though the problem is something altogether different; it just manifests itself in a string of frustrating squabbles. On the plus side, we might have a tidier bathroom and a crockery free appliance, but suffice to say the real issue is still there. Except now we're apparently upset because someone keeps taking charge of the TV remote...and so it goes.

In my view, it's better to be up front. We have to be able to discuss what we're really feeling and the reasons why. Of course, when it comes to more serious issues, this isn't always easy and quite often it means being as honest with ourselves as it does with our partner. But ultimately, if we really do want to create a recipe for a lasting, loving relationship, it's more than worth the effort.

What's the best writing advice you ever received?
If the protagonist(s) aren't aware, then neither is the reader.

I began my writing career penning scripts. When making the transition into novels, the best advice I ever received centered around *points of view.*

Understandable, considering in a script an actor can be doing one thing while something else takes place behind his back—an action that we, as an audience can see, but the protagonist can't. In novel writing, though, I don't have the luxury of a screen to play with. Everything has to be written from the protagonist's viewpoint.

Using the environment is one way of demonstrating what I mean. For example, if a protagonist walks into a room for the millionth time, would he or she really notice the ornament on the mantelpiece? I know when I walk into my living room, I don't take note of every single adornment...So that being the case, why would my characters?

However, some authors might want readers to know what a particular environment looks like. Settings are often pertinent, and we might need to give as much information as we can. But to simply describe a location is to take on the voice of a narrator, which in turn, pulls the reader out of our protagonist's head—something we writers certainly don't want to do.

So how do we get around this?

Well, if the aforementioned protagonist walks into the aforementioned room and the ornament is suddenly sitting on the table, then it's fair to say the character is going to notice and therefore check for other discrepancies. This enables us authors to then describe the room in more detail, introducing the information we need to impart, but in such a way that keeps the readers where they need to be— still inside the character's head.

Deborah Hughes: Yummy Soft Cookies

This recipe is from my Godmother. The cookies have a moist, cake-like quality to them. They're my favorite and now my husband's favorite cookie.

1-1/2 cups sugar
1/2 cup shortening
3-1/2 cups flour
2 eggs
2/3 cup milk
1 teaspoon vanilla extract
1 teaspoon baking soda
1/2 teaspoon salt
combination of raisins, butterscotch chips and chocolate chips (this combination is what makes these cookies special!)

Preheat oven to 350 degrees F.

Cream together shortening and sugar. Mix in eggs, then milk and vanilla extract.

In separate bowl, mix flour, baking soda, and salt. Slowly add to batter. Fold in equal quantities of raisins and chips, as much or as little as you like.

Drop by spoonfuls onto greased cookie sheet. Bake 12-15 minutes until the edges begin to brown.

Deborah Hughes and her family moved to a haunted old farmhouse when she was seven years old. That experience led to a lifelong exploration of the paranormal world. To escape her fears, Deborah told herself stories, and when she learned to write, she jotted them down. As time went on, she knew writing books was what she wanted to do. But, she ended up joining the Air Force, and that put her writing goals on hold for the next twenty years.

When her military career ended, Deborah turned her focus on producing books she loves to read. Her Tess Schafer-Medium series has supercharged her creative forces, and she can barely keep up with the urge to write them. She hopes her readers will gain some understanding of the paranormal world and most of all, enjoy a few hours of release from the stresses, fears, and demands of life. Read more about Deborah and her books at www.deborahjhughes.com.

What's your recipe for a lasting, loving relationship?
When I was a senior in high school, I took a Marriage Seminar through my church. It was a program designed to help teens understand what love and marriage were all about. One week the course was titled "Love is a Decision," and I rebelled against it. I just did not understand that at all. I considered love an emotion that we could not control...it was either there, or it wasn't. But I've since learned the error of that thinking!

We have to decide almost on a constant basis if we want to respond to a situation with love or with something that has nothing to do with love (such as anger, resentment, and hurt.) We have to decide what we want in a relationship on a constant basis. It's pretty much a given that at some point our loved ones are going to annoy us, disappoint us, and hurt us. When those situations arise, if we can consciously remember that we don't have to react impulsively but can take a moment to reason it out and decide to love, then things turn out a heck of a lot better for the relationship.

The thing to remember is that most often anger is a product of hurt or disappointment (usually because of an expectation not being met.) So now, when I am facing an angry person (especially my spouse!) I remind myself that they're acting out their hurt or responding to the fact that I have not met an expectation. Deciding to react with love always helps assuage some of the hurt and thus helps clear up the issue. On a side note: try not to expect so much; it will help ease your disappointments.

What's the best writing advice you ever received?
I read a line in Stephen King's book *On Writing* that said something like, "If we've been given a God-given talent then why in God's name aren't we using it?" and that just really hit me in the gut.

As writers we must know that storytelling is our God-given talent. We are compelled to write. We *must* write. We *need* to write. When I read that, it just struck me like a lightning bolt. I love to write. I have to write. So why the heck am I not going after my dream? After all, aside from writing, nothing gives me more pleasure than to share my stories with others. It's what we do when we create something; we want to share it. We are meant to share it. Creation of anything is meant to be shared. If we are inspired to create, then there's a reason for it, and what gives reason to it is the sharing of it.

So I read that line and wondered, what was I waiting for? I knew then and there that I needed to go after my dream and not worry about those who won't share in it. There are going to be plenty of others who will. Besides, I had God on my side. He gave me this ability to write, and I needed to be using it. So I stopped worrying about what others might think of my stories or my writing style and just went for it. And I don't regret that decision at all. Suddenly life became a heck of a lot more fun!

Cynthia Luhrs: Southern Tarts

1 egg, beaten
1 tablespoon butter, melted
1 teaspoon vanilla extract
1/2 cup pecans, chopped
3/4 cup brown sugar
phyllo dessert shells (from the freezer section)
1/2 cup chocolate chips (optional)

Preheat over to 350 degrees F.

Mix egg, butter, vanilla extract, pecans, and sugar together. Fill phyllo shells with mixture. Bake for 20 minutes.

Melt chocolate chips in microwave. Drizzle over warm tarts.

Store leftovers in an airtight container.

Cynthia Luhrs is the author of the Shadow Walkers novels. A graduate of Towson University, her Business degree serves her well now that she's an author and needs to stay organized. Prior to becoming an author, she toiled away in corporate America for many years. Her idea of a perfect day is no interruptions and the freedom to live in her head all day, writing to her heart's content, an icy cold drink next to her as she creates the next book. Of course her cats frequently disrupt this oasis of serenity. Read more about Cynthia and her books at www.cluhrs.com.

What's your recipe for a lasting, loving relationship?
Take one part laughter—laugh at yourself and with your loved ones.

Mix with two parts respect—respect others as you respect yourself.

Fold in a large dollop of humor— when an argument starts to spiral out of control, diffuse it with humor. I like to throw out a random thought. Something along the lines of, "I like turtles..." or "Do you think unicorns come in colors other than white?" Your loved one will be so taken aback by the odd statement, one or both of you will end up laughing and then be able to calmly discuss the issue.

Mix all ingredients well, then bake and enjoy a solid relationship for years to come.

What's the best writing advice you ever received?
The Four Supports of My Writing Cottage

Four? That's it? I know. It sounds like a rather small list doesn't it? But together these posts form the foundation for all writers to build a lasting career.

1. Be a reader.

2. Read books in the same genre you write. Notice the books you put down after a page or a chapter. Why? For good books read first for pleasure. Then read a second time to figure out why you liked that particular book so much. Was it the snappy dialogue? The characters? The overall story? What was it about the book that kept you up all night reading and long after you finished it, you kept thinking about a character, message, or story?

3. Learn the industry and your craft. Keep learning and improving. Your first book should make you cringe after you've written the third and so on. Keep up with the movers and shakers on social media. Take classes, read books on writing, talk to other authors.

4. Listen to your readers. They'll tell you what they love and dislike about your story. If you hear the same feedback from more than three readers, it's something you might consider changing.

Now that you have a solid foundation, it's time to add the cottage. My cottage is built out of books. Well, maybe an eReader, so it's a tiny cottage, but it holds my entire library.

Never stop reading.

Judy Baker: Tasty Doggie Biscuits

My recipe comes from my love of dogs. I've had dogs all my life, most of the time, more than one. But now I only have a fourteen-year-old Airedale who's receiving all my care and love. These biscuits will not only be a treat for your dog but will help keep his teeth clean.

3-1/2 cups all-purpose flour
2 cups whole-wheat flour
1 cup rye flour
1 cup cornmeal
2 cups cracked wheat (bulgur)
1/2 cup nonfat dry milk
1 tablespoon salt (or less)
1 package dry yeast dissolved in 1/4 cup warm water
1 pint chicken stock (once in a while I'll add beef stock instead of chicken)
1 egg
1 tablespoon milk

Note: My dog is fourteen years old, so I also add a small drop of liquid vitamins. Also, if your dog is an older dog or has special needs, do like I did and asked you veterinarian if you should add or delete any substance from the biscuit recipe, especially if your dog is allergic to anything on the list.

Preheat oven to 300 degrees F.

In a large bowl combine the dry ingredients. Add dissolved yeast and stock. In a separate bowl beat egg and milk together. Add to mixture. Mix all ingredients, then knead dough.

Roll dough to 1/4" thickness. Use dog bone shaped cookie cutter to cut biscuits. Place biscuits on cookie sheet. Bake for 45 minutes. Turn off oven, but leave biscuits in oven overnight. Biscuits will be hard the next morning.

Judy Baker writes historical western suspense romances under her own name and contemporary romance and romantic suspense as Anna Sugg. Most of her books include a dog as a character, especially her contemporary books. In the Yellow Creek series, *Secret Past* has a Dalmatian and *Ghost Thunder* has a Brittney Spaniel, while her historical westerns have a wolf-dog. Her next Yellow Creek book will have a rare breed—a mutt who travels back in time to be with the heroine. Books in her Silver Sage Creek series include *Better She Die*, *Better She Live*, and *Better She Love*. Read more about Judy/Anna and her books at www.judybaker.coffeecup.com and www.anna_sugg.coffeecup.com.

What's your recipe for a lasting, loving relationship?

My hubby and I have been married for almost forty-three years, and I would say the recipe for this lasting, loving relationship is respect for each other as individuals. He is my best friend, and we do almost everything together. We go on adventurous vacations, have morning coffee together, kiss each other goodbye in the mornings before going off to work, talk over a glass of wine, listen to each other, enjoy family gatherings, and laugh a lot. We also give each other space and support to follow our own dreams. Without him giving me my own space to write, I would never have written my first book. We support each other for being who we are.

What's the best writing advice you ever received?

Get the story out of your head and the words onto a white sheet of paper. Don't stop until it's done. When I heard that advice, I did it—finished my first manuscript. Sure, it was a mess, but DONE. I was so proud of myself. But, don't stop; learn how to make it better. Perseverance is the key to keep moving forward.

Alicia Dean: Easy Cheesecake

8 ounce brick cream cheese, softened
1/2 cup granulated sugar
2 eggs
1/2 teaspoon vanilla extract.
ready-made graham cracker pie crust

Preheat oven to 350 degrees F.

Beat together cream cheese and sugar. Add one egg and beat until blended. Add second egg and beat until blended. Add vanilla extract and beat until blended.

Pour into pie crust. Bake for approximately 35-40 minutes. Oven temperatures vary, so after about 30 minutes, check the cheesecake every five minutes or so. It's done when small brown spots and/or cracks start appearing on the surface. Remove from oven when there are only a few brown spots. Cool, then refrigerate for 3 hours before serving. Add topping of your choice.

Alicia Dean lives in Edmond, Oklahoma. She has three grown children and a huge network of supportive friends and family. She writes mostly contemporary suspense (*Death Notice*) and paranormal (*Liberty Awakened.*) but has also written in other genres, including vintage-set historicals (the 1920s-set *Ruined*, releasing in the fall of 2014 and the 1950s-set *End of Lonely Street*, releasing January 7, 2015.)

Other than reading and writing, her passions are Elvis Presley, MLB, NFL (she usually works in a mention of one or all three into her stories,) and watching her favorite television shows such as *Vampire Diaries*, *Justified*, and *Dexter* (Even though it has sadly ended, she will forever be a fan.) Read more about Alicia and her books at www.aliciadean.com.

What's your recipe for a lasting, loving relationship?
I am divorced and have never had a romantic lasting, loving relationship, so I will have to speak to the relationships with family and friends. My recipe is to show you care about them by being there when they need you. Even if it's just to check on their well being or to send a card. Knowing that someone cares is comforting in times of need. I feel it's important to take interest in their lives and to really listen to them, even if you're not particularly invested in the topic.

I have a close and loving relationship with my grown kids, my siblings, and several other family members, and with many, many friends. I love people, and I try to show that love as often as I can. (Actually, it's odd that I love people, because I am also somewhat of a hermit, but then, that's the writer in me, I suppose.)

My very best friend and I have been friends for more than forty years, since the seventh grade. We actually have very little in common as far as interests. She's not a TV fanatic, an Elvis fanatic, or an MLB fanatic like I am. However, our senses of humor are very similar, and we do have a few commonalties. But I love and respect her almost more than anyone else on Earth. I think mainly the way to a lasting, loving relationship of any kind is to treat others like you would want to be treated. Simple, yes, but it works.

What's the best writing advice you ever received?
I have received a ton of good writing advice over the years, but the first advice I ever received that made me know I could do this, that I could be a writer, was from my instructor, who later became my friend, Mel Odom. I took a class with Mel in 2001. I had always wanted to write and had dabbled but had never completed a novel. I told Mel I was overwhelmed at the idea of writing an entire book, and he said, "Then write one scene at a time."

That seems pretty obvious and simplistic, but it was as though a light bulb switched on in my brain. I could do that. I could write one scene. And then another. And another. And so on, until I linked them together into a complete novel. Since then, I have completed over twenty novels and short stories. That advice still rings true. When I'm starting a new project, or when I hit a wall, I think, "Okay, write one scene at a time." But, if that scene isn't working, move on to the next. And, eventually, scene by scene, good or bad, you WILL finish.

Which brings me to another excellent piece of advice: Give yourself permission to write crap. No one has to see your work until you're ready, so just get the story down, no matter how poorly written. You will be surprised when you go back through, how much better it is than you thought. Then you simply work on polishing. Each time you go through the story, it will get better, but you must reach a point where you let go. If you continue to revise, you will never move forward. Know when it's time to send it out. Then start on your next story.

Leslie Langtry: Chocolate Twinkie Cake

My mom came up with this one. There have been Twinkie cakes out there for a long time, but they all involved bananas or other fruit. Mom thought it would be better with chocolate. The first time she made it just with melted chocolate chips, but she didn't like the consistency. Then she added the eggs (cuz she's awesome that way,) and it was perfect. Sometimes she tops it with crushed toffee, nuts, M&M's or chocolate syrup or really, anything. I make this recipe every time I finish writing a book.

1 box of Twinkies (about 8 or 9 total)
6 ounces chocolate chips
2 tablespoons water
4 eggs
12 ounce tub of Cool Whip

Slice Twinkies lengthwise and lay both halves in a glass pan, filling side up.

Melt the chocolate chips with the water in microwave for 1 minute.

Separate the egg yolks from the egg whites. Add yolks only to melted chocolate. Allow to cool.

Beat the egg whites until they form foamy peaks. Add the egg whites to the chocolate and egg yolks and mix. Pour over the top of the Twinkies. Go slowly first, making sure you cover the Twinkies—then go back and pour the rest, filling in the spaces.

Spread Cool Whip carefully over the top. Use as much or as little as you want. I use the whole thing. Cover with foil or plastic wrap and refrigerate for at least four hours before serving. Always refrigerate the cake you don't eat.

Leslie Langtry is the author of the comedy/mystery series about the Bombay Family of Assassins, including *'Scuse Me While I Kill This Guy*, and the romantic comedy *Sex, Lies & Family Vacations*.

Leslie lives in the Midwest with her husband, two teenagers (who keep insisting she's their mother,) and a menagerie of cats, dogs, parakeets and guinea pigs, who don't care who she is as long as she feeds them. Read more about Leslie and her books at www.leslielangtry.com.

What's your recipe for a lasting, loving relationship?

My husband and I are celebrating our twenty-fifth anniversary this fall. Somehow, we've made it this far without any serious bumps in the road. I think the reason for this is that we've always let each other take risks and do what we love career-wise. He's traveled a lot for his job over the years with no complaints from me, and he encouraged me to quit my job to see if I could sell a book and become a novelist. And even though this makes things difficult financially (especially when you have two kids,) we've always made it work. As a result, we feel like we followed our dreams and have no regrets. And our kids see us doing what we love and realize that they can do that, too, (which is good because our daughter wants to be a professional trumpet musician.) Our philosophy is if you aren't happy with what you do for a living, you won't be happy in your relationship or anything else.

Other than that, you MUST have a sense of humor. That's a requirement. Well, that and good hygiene. You should never overlook hygiene.

What's the best writing advice you ever received?

"I can fix a broken page. I can't fix a blank one." Attributed to Nora Roberts. I heard this at a Romance Writers of America conference, and it is the most important advice I heed and share with other writers. You don't have to "wait for the muse to visit" or even be in the "correct frame of mind" to write (That one makes me laugh because I've never been there. I think it's a place you can only go if you abuse absinthe.) Just get something down on paper. When you look at it later, you can fix it, rewrite it or even delete it. But you have to start it. I've never been a big believer in "writer's block." You can always write. It might be crap, but it's writing. Believe me, I've written some real crap pages over the years. But I've always been able to fix them.

AND— *"Dickens didn't write what people wanted. Dickens wanted what people wanted."* – G.K. Chesterton. As a writer of popular fiction, I think it's completely true. I started out trying to write historical romance because that's what my friends wrote, and that's what I thought people wanted. It sucked. It totally sucked. I tried two more times and those books sucked. Then I wrote what I wanted for fun, and that was the book that sold. I always write what I want to read.

You shouldn't deconstruct bestsellers and write to a formula you think will sell. It never works. Readers are too smart for that. You have to find your own voice and write what you want to. There is no "magic formula"—there's only you. Unless you have a clone. If you have a clone, call me. Because I want one.

Janis Susan May: Chocolate Sin

This is a flourless chocolate mousse cake.

1/2 cup sugar

1/2 cup water

1 stick butter, cut in pieces, plus small amount of melted butter to grease pan

12 ounces semi or bittersweet chocolate bits

6 large eggs

1/4 cup dark rum or raspberry or orange liqueur (or orange juice if you want cake non-alcoholic)

Preheat oven to 325 degrees F.

Brush 8" round cake pan with melted butter. Line bottom with parchment or wax paper.

Bring sugar and water to boil. Add butter and chocolate. Whisk all around in pan until butter and chocolate melt. Remove from heat. Fairly quickly whisk in eggs until absorbed. Don't overbeat! Add rum, liqueur, or orange juice.

Pour batter into cake pan. Place pan in a roasting pan. Add water to the roasting pan (a la bain-marie.) Bake 45 minutes for a dense, moist, almost fudge-like consistency. Bake 1 hour for a slightly drier, but still quite moist cake. For a thick, dry, chewy texture, bake 1-1/2 hours, but keep an eye on the cake to prevent burning. Also, watch the water level. Add more water if necessary, but use boiling water, not cold.

Allow to cool, then unmold onto a serving plate. For presentation, you can sprinkle the top with confectioner's sugar, sprinkling over a lacy doily, then carefully removing the doily to create a lovely pattern. Other suggested toppings: frost with whipped cream or sweetened crème fraiche, topping with fresh raspberries or other suitable fresh fruit, curls of white chocolate, or an artistic sprinkling of white chocolate chips, chopped peppermint candies, white or milk chocolate leaves to contrast with the dark chocolate of the cake, candied violets, or a light dusting of fleurs de sel.

Janis Susan May not only writes both romance and horror but also children's books as Janis Susan Patterson, cozy mysteries as Janis Patterson, and scholarly and non-fiction works as JSM Patterson. She is one of the original founders of Romance Writers of America and has served several times on the Regional Board of Mystery Writers of America, as well as being a member of Novelists Inc., the Authors Guild, and Sisters in Crime. She has set records for re-releasing some of her backlist in a publishing blitz where she brought out a book every two weeks from June 30 to October 30, 2014. In the past she has been an actress, a singer, a jewelry designer, editor-in-chief of two multi-magazine publishing companies, and Supervisor of Accessioning in a bio-genetic DNA lab—among other things.

Janis and her husband, a retired Navy officer, are both avid amateur Egyptologists. They live in Texas with an assortment of rescued fur babies. Read more about Janis and her books at www.JanisSusanMay.com.

What's your recipe for a lasting, loving relationship?
Pick the right person. Then be the right person. If both husband and wife each give just a little more than they get, it's a great relationship. And never go to bed angry. Stay in love. That can be work at times, but it's worth it. Remember, you're not perfect either! The Southern woman's advice for a wife was to prop your man up on one side and lean against him on the other. If both partners do this, it's great. Balance your strengths and weaknesses. Kiss a lot. Hold hands in public.

What's the best writing advice you ever received?
Finish the book. Then rewrite it until it's perfect...or as close as humanly possible. Take pride in your work—it will outlive you, and people you never met will judge you by it. Be accurate. Learn proper spelling and grammar and use them. Writing is a profession deserving of the same application and respect as any other. It's not easy just because you can do it in your pajamas!

Mitzi Flyte: All-Alone-Make-Me-Feel-Better Rejection Brownie in a Cup

Make this recipe whenever you feel down and need to feel better.

2 tablespoons butter or margarine, melted
2 tablespoons Amaretto
dash of salt
4 tablespoons sugar (you can use Truvia for Baking but why would you since you've been rejected)
2 tablespoons unsweetened cocoa powder
4 tablespoons all-purpose flour

In a 12 ounce coffee mug (preferably a clean one) mix together the Amaretto, melted butter, and salt. Add cocoa powder and mix. Use up that anger at your rejection. Add sugar (use more anger-power.) Add flour (final mix.)

Microwave for 60-90 seconds. The center will be gooey. It's supposed to be. But it's HOT! So let it cool. I know it's hard to wait, but have a bit of Amaretto. Enjoy. Then get back to writing.

Mitzi Flyte has been writing for publication since her first rejection at age twelve, for a short story she sent off to *Family Circle*. She's a retired RN, now writing fulltime. She's published horror and mystery short stories, erotic romance, children's short stories, poetry, and personal essays.

Mitzi lives in rural Pennsylvania with her writer husband, daughter, dopey dog, and assorted cats. Read more about Mitzi and her writing at www.mitziflyte.com.

What's your recipe for a lasting, loving relationship?

Interesting question for me since I was divorced for more than thirty years and recently remarried two years ago at the age of sixty-four. I found a gentleman who had similar likes. He's also a writer, so he understands. We forgive each other everything and always say, "I love you" before going to sleep. I believe that recognizing each other's needs is the most important thing. That and encouragement. Even though we're retired, our interests keep us busy.

What's the best writing advice you ever received?
That came from Eileen Charbonneau who said to "stick your heroine up a tree and keep throwing stones at her." And to stick with it. Perseverance is the one thing every writer needs. That and some Amaretto and chocolate.

Ruby Merritt: Creamy Frozen Fruit Salad

2 cups of sour cream
2 tablespoon lemon juice
3/4 cup sugar
1/8 teaspoon salt
1 banana, sliced
8 ounce can crushed pineapple, drained
1/4 cup sliced maraschino cherries

Mix all together and freeze in individual desserts cups. Thaw 5 minutes before serving.

Ruby Merritt is a teacher and an author who writes stories because they won't leave her alone until she does. Her debut novel and first book in her Spirited Heart series, *Ella's Choice*, takes place in 1870s Wyoming. Read more about Ruby and her writing at www.RubyMerrittAuthor.com.

What's your recipe for a lasting, loving relationship?
Always treat your partner as you would want to be treated.

What's the best writing advice you ever received?
Read voraciously. Write passionately.

Brenda Novak: Caramel Apples

The best caramel I've ever tasted! I make these every Halloween. My family LOVES them! Serves 6.

1 cup sugar
3/4 cup white corn syrup
1 can sweetened condensed milk
1/8 teaspoon salt
1/4 cup butter
1 teaspoon vanilla extract
6 medium-sized apples

Cook sugar, corn syrup, sweetened condensed milk, and salt over medium heat to soft-ball stage. Remove from heat and let cool slightly. Stir in butter and vanilla extract. Quickly dip 6 med-sized apples and place on waxed paper.

Brenda Novak is a *New York Times* & *USA Today* bestselling author of more than fifty books. A four-time RITA nominee, she has won many awards, including the National Reader's Choice, the Bookseller's Best, the Book Buyer's Best, the Daphne, and the Holt Medallion. She also runs an annual on-line auction for diabetes research every May at *www.brendanovak.com* (Her youngest son has this disease.) To date, she's raised nearly $2.5 million. Read more about Brenda and her books at www.brendanovak.com.

What's your recipe for a lasting, loving relationship?
Avoid negative thought patterns. Allowing yourself to mentally or verbally tear down your significant other is like gnawing at the bond that holds you together.

What's the best writing advice you ever received?
Write fearlessly. I *love* that. It tells me to write what I want to write and to enjoy the process, even if I only please myself.

Shelley Noble: Christmas Divinity

Divinity MUST be made on a dry day or it won't harden. Do not attempt on a humid day. The egg white mixture MUST be beaten continually once you begin.

2 cups sugar
1/2 cup Karo Light Corn Syrup
1/3 cup water
2 egg whites
1 teaspoon vanilla extract
1 cup chopped pecans
pecan halves (optional)

Place sugar, syrup, and water in a heavy pan. Boil until sugar is dissolved and liquid is clear.

In a large bowl, beat egg whites with an electric mixer until stiff. Add 1/3 of hot liquid to egg whites, beating constantly. (Remember, egg whites must be beaten continuously through the rest of the process.)

Return liquid to heat and cook until it spins a good thread. Add 1/3 more of hot liquid to egg whites, beating constantly. Continue beating and return liquid to heat and cook until it makes a hard brittle ball when dropped in cold water. Pour remainder of liquid into egg whites and continue beating. When it thickens, continue to beat by hand. When the mixture begins to hold its shape, add vanilla extract and nuts.

Quickly drop by teaspoonful onto waxed paper before the mixture hardens. Can be garnished with a pecan half if so desired. Let set. It will melt in your mouth.

Shelley Noble is a *New York Times* bestselling author of women's fiction. Her novels include *Beach Colors, Stargazey Point,* and *Breakwater Bay.* Tie-in novellas include *Holidays at Crescent Cove, Stargazey Nights, Newport Dreams, and A Breakwater Christmas Wedding.*

As Shelley Freydont she writes the Liv Montgomery, Celebration Bay Festival Mysteries for Berkley Prime Crime and the upcoming Newport Gilded Age Mysteries beginning with *A Gilded Grave*.

A former professional dancer and choreographer, she most recently worked on the films *Mona Lisa Smile* and *The Game Plan*. Shelley lives at the Jersey shore and loves to discover new beaches and indulge her passion for lighthouses and vintage carousels. Read more about Shelley and her books at www.shelleynoble.com and www.shelleyfreydont.com.

What's your recipe for a lasting, loving relationship?
In the words of Johnny Mercer, *"Accentuate the positive, eliminate the negative and don't mess with Mr. In-Between."*

What's the best writing advice you ever received?
Write with your heart, and practice, practice, practice to make each work the best it can be. I try to keep that advice always in my mind. Nothing about marketing or publicity or how to make it on Facebook, but advice about the actual writing, about perfecting your craft, something that sometimes gets lost in the hoopla.

Renee Field: Charlie's Favorite

1 cup butter, soften
1-1/2 cups brown sugar
1/2 cup granulated sugar
2 egg yolks
1 tablespoon water
1 teaspoon vanilla extract
2-1/2 cups flour
1/2 teaspoon baking soda
1 package chocolate chips
3 egg whites
1 teaspoon cream of tartar

Preheat oven to 350 degrees F.

Mix together butter, 1/2 cup brown sugar, granulated sugar, and egg yolks. Add 1 tablespoon water and 1 teaspoon vanilla extract. Add the flour and baking soda.

Spread batter in a greased 9"x13" pan. Sprinkle chocolate chips over batter and gently press into batter.

Beat egg whites with cream of tartar. Slowly add remaining brown sugar to make a soft meringue mixture. Spread meringue over the batter.

Bake for 20 minutes. Allow to cool before cutting into squares.

Renee Field not only writes in multiple genres, she promotes other authors on StoryFinds.com, a site she founded in 2012 to help support indie authors. Among the various genres in which Renee writes are erotic romance for Ellora's Cave & HQN Spice Briefs, sensual paranormal romance as an indie author, and new adult romance. In addition, she writes nitty-gritty young adult and paranormal young adult romance novels under the pen name Renee

Pace.

Renee calls Halifax, Nova Scotia, Canada home and loves her view of the Atlantic Ocean. She juggles work and four children and is a firm believer in soul-mates and the power of the sea. Read more about Renee and her books at www.reneefield.com and www.reneepace.com.

What's your recipe for a lasting, loving relationship?
Treat each other with respect. Love is wonderful but if you don't find your partner a friend, then it won't last. A friend is the person you tell your darkest secrets to, and a friend is there for you when you're sick and need help. I've been married twenty-three years, and he's still my BFF. My hubby is the first person I call when I get good news and the first when I get bad news. We continue to say the key polite words to each other—like when he cooks super, I make a point of saying, "Thanks so much, dear, and I'll clean up," and he does the same.

Also, men and women do think differently. Long ago I gave up ever thinking my hubby would see the "dirt" in our house that needed to be cleaned. I learned early on that what I perceive as dirty and what he sees are two entirely different things, but if I ask him to help, he never hesitates to clean a washroom, and when you have four children, that's key.

In addition, don't go to bed mad. It's true. If you have to stay up until two in the morning (and yes we've done this,) talk it through. You will both feel better in the morning without that angry feeling hanging over your head. I'm a firm believer that negative energy needs to be stamped out ASAP.

And finally, make the time to be with your hubby. Plan a once a year getaway with just him and you—even if it's only an hour away. For us this became key when our fourth child was born, and it certainly has helped to rejuvenate our marriage. We now look forward to our three day/four night getaways from our children, and we don't feel guilty. This is a mental health break, and it's important to ensure you'll still want to be with your partner when all the children leave the nest.

What's the best writing advice you ever received?

Keep on writing. It's simple. Like any craft you'll only get better with more practice. And don't write for what's popular. Write what you want to write. If you don't love your writing, I'm a firm believer no one else will. Also, join a local writing group. You'll gain more insight to your craft and the business of writing. And be prepared to be critiqued. Critique partners are key to helping you hone your craft and book.

The best thing about writing today is you don't need to wait for a BIG publisher. Don't be afraid to go the indie route and publish on your own.

Kathryn Quick: Healthy S'mores Bars

This recipe is eggless, low in sugar, and gluten-free.

4 tablespoons coconut oil
1 tablespoon unsweetened almond milk
1 teaspoon butter extract
1/2 teaspoon salt
1-1/2 cups graham cracker crumbs
1/2 cup maple syrup (the real stuff)
2 packets Knox unflavored gelatin
6 tablespoons cold water
1 tablespoon light coconut milk
1-1/2 ounces dark chocolate

Preheat oven to 350 degrees F.

In microwave-safe bowl, add 3 tablespoons coconut oil, almond milk, butter extract, and 1/4 teaspoon salt. Microwave at 20-second intervals, stirring between each, until everything is melted. Stir in the graham cracker crumbs.

Line an 8" brownie pan with parchment paper both ways. Scoop the graham cracker mixture into the pan and press firmly. Bake for 10 minutes, then let cool completely.

In a microwave-safe bowl, add the gelatin and water. Microwave at 20-second intervals, stirring between each, until the gelatin dissolves.

Add the maple syrup and 1/4 teaspoon salt to a stand mixer bowl with whisk attachment. With mixer on medium, slowly add the gelatin mixture. Whip on high until white, thick, and glossy (approximately 12 minutes.) Scoop over the cooled graham cracker crust. (Any extra marshmallow mixture can be spooned onto a sheet of parchment paper and left to sit overnight.)

In a microwave-safe bowl, add the coconut milk and remaining coconut oil.

Microwave at 15-second intervals, stirring between each until melted. Add the chocolate and microwave again at 15-second intervals.

Allow chocolate to cool until just slightly warm, then spread over the marshmallow layer.

Kathryn Quick was born long ago in Shenandoah, Pennsylvania and has been writing since the Sisters in St. Casmir's Grammar School gave her the ruled yellow paper and a Number Two pencil. She writes contemporary and career romances, romantic comedies, and historical romances, as well as urban fantasy (as P. K. Eden with writing partner Patt Mihailoff for Berkley.)

Kathryn is one of the founding members of Liberty States Fiction Writers, a multi-genre writers' organization dedicated to furthering the craft of writing and helping aspiring writers become published.

Her upcoming releases include The Bachelor's Three series (*Bachelor.com, Solid Gold Bachelor,* and *The Bachelor's Agenda*) and as P.K. Eden, *The Mirror*, part of The Grimm Protectors urban fantasy series. Read more about Kathryn and her books at www.kathrynquick.com.

What's your recipe for a lasting, loving relationship?
You need three things:
Interests of your own
Interests of his own
Interests you share together

The first two are used to have something to talk about when you are together for the third.

What's the best writing advice you ever received?
My father, who was the smartest man in the universe although he only had an eighth grade education (he lied about his age to volunteer for WWII) told me, "Quitting is what you do right before you were going to succeed."

Susan Cory: Killer Tiramisu

The Spa Version—only 275 calories per serving. Make the day before serving and freeze overnight. Serves 16.

4 eggs, separated
3/4 cup sugar
6 ounces soft Neufchatel cheese
6 ounces mascarpone cheese
1 teaspoon vanilla extract
1 cup heavy cream
1/2 cup light cream
1/2 cup strong coffee
20 ladyfingers
1/4 cup Amaretto (optional)
3/4 cup dark chocolate, broken into pieces
1/2 cup half-and-half
1/4 cup nonfat milk
1/4 cup non-sweetened cocoa powder

Spray 9" x 12" sheet pan with Pam. Line with wax paper. Spray bottom again.

Mix together egg yolks and 1/2 cup of sugar on high for 2 minutes. Add Neufchatel cheese, mascarpone, and vanilla extract. Whip until smooth and set aside.

Whip heavy cream and light cream until medium peaks form, then fold gently into yolk-cheese mixture. Do not over-mix.

Whip egg whites into soft peaks and add remaining 1/4 cup sugar, whipping until medium peaks form. Fold egg whites
into the yolk-cheese base. Cover and refrigerate until ready to assemble.

Assemble ladyfingers across bottom of pan in two rows. Pour coffee (with optional Amaretto) over ladyfingers. Pour mousse mixture over top and smooth the surface. Refrigerate for 30 minutes.

While the cake is cooling, bring the half-and-half and milk to a simmer in a pan. Pour over the broken-up chocolate in a bowl and let sit for 1 minute, then stir until smooth. Allow to cool.

Pour topping over cake to cover without using a tool (just tip pan.) Sprinkle with sifted cocoa and freeze for 8 hours.

Allow to sit for thirty minutes at room temperature before serving.

Susan Cory lives in Cambridge, Massachusetts and works as a residential architect. She grew up in New Jersey, devouring mysteries and loved seeing order restored by ingenious sleuths. But the visual arts were her medium of expression. At architecture school at Harvard's G.S.D., she discovered a setting just ripe for murder. She couldn't understand why there were no mysteries about architecture students doing each other in. So she decided to remedy this oversight.

Forgetting she was a "Vizzie," not a "Verbie," she spent several years getting up to speed with the using-words-thing. *Conundrum* is an ode to her profession and all the deviously clever practitioners within it. The first ode. Iris Reid, her protagonist, will find herself tossed into any number of tight spots as the series progresses. Read more about Susan and her writing at www.susancory.com.

What's your recipe for a lasting, loving relationship?
My recipe for creating a lasting relationship—in a partner or a friend—is to first find someone who shares your sense of humor.

What's the best writing advice you ever received?
My favorite writing advice comes from Anne Lamott: *"You own everything that happened to you. Tell your stories. If people wanted you to write warmly about them, they should've behaved better."*

Judy Penz Sheluk: Lemon Blueberry Pudding Cake

1 package lemon cake mix
1 box of instant lemon pudding mix
4 eggs
1-1/4 cups milk
3 tablespoons vegetable oil
1 cup fresh blueberries
1 lemon
1 tablespoon butter, melted
1 cup icing sugar
pinch of salt

Preheat oven to 350 degrees F.

Coat the blueberries with a little cake mix. This will keep them from sinking to the bottom of the cake.

Combine remaining cake mix, pudding mix, eggs, milk, and vegetable oil in mixer bowl and mix for five minutes on medium speed. Fold blueberries into the batter.

Pour into greased pan and bake 40-60 minutes, depending on pan size. Allow to cool.

To make glaze, mix the juice from 1 lemon, melted butter, salt, and enough icing sugar to create a proper pouring consistency. Pour over top of cake.

Judy Penz Sheluk is a freelance writer whose work has been published in dozens of U.S. and Canadian publications. She is also the senior editor of *New England Antiques Journal* and the editor of *Home BUILDER Magazine Canada*. In her more mysterious pursuits, Judy is the author of *The Hanged Man's Noose*, an amateur sleuth mystery set to debut in July 2015 from Barking Rain Press. She also has two short stories coming out in anthologies in

November 2014: "PLAN D," will appear in *The Whole She-Bang 2*, and "Live Free or Die" will appear in *EFD2: World Enough and Crime*. Read more about Judy and her writing at www.judypenzsheluk.com.

What's your recipe for a lasting, loving relationship?

Trust and respect each another. Without trust and respect, you don't have a relationship.

What's the best writing advice you ever received?

Make time to write every day. The writing muscle is like any other muscle; the more you exercise it, the stronger it becomes.

Kay Manis: Mam-Maw's Banana Nut Bread

An old recipe straight from my grandmother (Her name also just happens to be the pen name for one of my upcoming novels) It's not technically a dessert, but I always eat it for dessert.

2 cups sifted flour
2 eggs
1 teaspoon baking soda
1 teaspoon vanilla extract
1/2 teaspoon salt
1/2 cup butter, melted
1 cup sugar
4 small ripe bananas, mashed
1 cup chopped nuts (optional)

Preheat oven to 350 degrees F.

Mix all dry ingredients. Mix wet ingredients into the dry mixture until blended. Pour batter into greased and floured loaf pan. Bake 55-60 minutes until center is cooked.

Kay Manis writes adult contemporary romance. *Skater Boy* and *My Skater Boy* are the first two books in her X-Treme Boys series. She loves her experience as an indie author.

Kay lives in Austin, Texas with her husband of over twenty years, their eighteen-year-old daughter, and ten-year-old Chihuahua Tiny. When not reading or writing, she's eating out with friends or napping. Look for *Moto Boy* and *My Moto Boy*, the next two books in her series, coming soon. Read more about Kay and her books at www.kaymanis.com.

What's your recipe for a lasting, loving relationship?
For marriage, it's all about finding the right person. No amount of counseling can fix a relationship if you're involved with the wrong kind of mate. Find

someone who makes you laugh from the start. Marriage is full of ups and downs and lots of in-betweens. Romance comes and goes, heat flames and diminishes, but someone who can make you laugh will get you through it all.

What's the best writing advice you ever received?

I have a book in which I collect authors' signatures along with their best advice for an indie author like me. By far, the majority of the authors write two things for me.

1. Don't give up...ever!
2. Write for you, only you; write the story YOU love.

Caridad Pineiro: Cuban Flan

Why a Cuban Flan recipe? Well, first, because I'm Cuban-American. Second, I have the world's worst sweet tooth. I think meals should begin with dessert and only then proceed to anything else. Unfortunately, I haven't been able to convince others of that.

I learned to make flan from my grandmother. Her process for making the caramel was like making candy, resulting in a sweet caramel that's lighter in color— actually clear if you don't want to push the cooking.

1 cup plain white sugar
6 whole eggs
6 egg yolks
1 cup whole milk
1 can sweetened condensed milk (Magnolia or Eagle Brand are favorites!)
2 teaspoons vanilla extract

Preheat oven to 350 degrees F.

Place a large baking pan filled halfway with hot, but not boiling, water in the oven. This will make what is called a bain-marie. The bain-marie will help keep the flan from drying out and will allow it to cook evenly.

Start with 1/2 cup of sugar and dissolve it in 1/2 cup to 1 cup water. Make sure the sugar is fully dissolved before you begin to heat it. If you have any sugar left, it will form crystals and be gritty. Once the sugar is dissolved, set the pan with the sugar over medium heat in a heavy medium/small saucepan or preferably, an ovenproof dish. Use a wooden spoon to stir until the sugar water is reduced (It should get thicker as it cooks.) Grandma liked it light, but you can let it get golden and keep on going until it is a dark brown. (*Be very careful!* Cooked sugar is very hot and can burn the skin if it spatters.)

If you did not use an ovenproof pan/dish, quickly pour the hot caramel syrup into an ungreased baking dish. Swirl the pan until the sugar coats the bottom and sides of the pan/dish. The caramel will start to harden at this point. When you cook the flan in the oven, the caramel will melt and create a syrup that the flan will swim in.

Gently mix together the eggs and egg yolks. Do not create too much froth or bubbles as these will linger and ruin the texture of the flan. Add the condensed milk and gently mix a little more. Then add the rest of the regular whole milk (for ease and to get all the condensed milk, put the whole milk into the can and use it to wash out the thick condensed milk that lingers in the can.) Gently stir until the mixture is smooth. Add the vanilla extract.

Pour egg/milk custard mixture into the baking dish (make sure the caramel has set against the sides and bottom of the pan.)
Set this baking dish into the larger baking pan. Add boiling water to the baking pan until it is about halfway up the side of the dish with the flan mixture.

Bake 35-40 minutes until a knife inserted into the center comes out clean. If it's a little soft (but not runny,) that's okay as it will continue to cook for a bit. Let the flan cool in the water. After half an hour or so, remove the flan from the bain-marie and refrigerate for at least an hour or more.

It's actually preferable to make the flan the day before and let it sit overnight so the caramel soaks into the outermost layer. Before serving, run a sharp knife around the edge of the flan to release it from the baking dish. Place a larger serving plate (preferably with a small lip to keep the caramel liquid from spilling) over the baking dish, and invert the flan onto the serving platter. Keep refrigerated until it is time to serve the flan.

For simple variations, you can add a little Amaretto or Grand Marnier to both the caramel and the custard mix. For more complex variations, try a chocolate flan. One delicious variation is to increase the number of egg yolks and eliminate the egg whites entirely. This will make a very thick rich egg custard called Toscinillo del Cielo.

Caridad Pineiro is a *New York Times* and *USA Today* bestselling author and Jersey Girl who just wants to write, travel, and spend more time with family and friends. She's the author of over 40 novels/novellas and loves romance novels, super heroes, TV and cooking. Read more about Caridad at www.caridad.com.

What's your recipe for a lasting, loving relationship?
Like a recipe, a relationship may take time to get just right. The trick is to keep on trying until you get just the right mix of ingredients. It's hard work at times, but hopefully worth all that effort.

What's the best writing advice you ever received?
Successful people don't focus on what others are doing. They focus on their own goals and how to accomplish them. Set defined goals in order to accomplish defined results. I know that's tough in the publishing world because of all the variables, but don't give up. Mary Pickford once said, *"Failure is not the falling down. It's the not getting up."*

Kathryn Jane: Guilt-Free Fun!

Simple, fat free, guilt free, smooth, and delicious. Great for everyday, or easily dressed up for a special occasion. This recipe makes four servings of about 200 calories each, and these aren't empty calories!

1 package any flavor Jell-O
1 cup boiling water
1 cup Greek yogurt

Mix one package of your favorite Jell-O with a cup of boiling water. Stir well and allow to stand until room temp. Add one cup of plain, fat free, Greek yogurt and whisk until smooth. Refrigerate until set (usually about 2 hours.)

Options:
Variations are endless. Step it up a notch by using vanilla flavored yogurt. Add fruit, coconut, nuts, or even marshmallows. Swirl two flavors into a dish together, or layer for color fun. Pour into popsicle molds for a great frozen treat.

Kathryn Jane is an award-winning author who loves writing about kick-ass women—the kind she'd like to hang out with. Smart, self-reliant, think-on-their-feet ladies who are just as happy eating a loaded hot dog at a ballgame as they are sipping champagne in the back of a limo. Women who laugh as hard as they cry, love good sweaty sex, don't understand the appeal of perfection, and can keep secrets.

Her heroes are tough, hot, inherently kind, and often baffled by the opposite sex.

Addicted to the ocean, Kathryn lives on the west coast of Canada with two obnoxious cats and a faithful dog to keep the man of her dreams company while she's busy penning fast-paced adventures about stubborn women and the men who dare to love them. Titles in her Intrepid Women series include *Do Not Tell Me No, Touch Me, Daring to Love,* and *Voices.* Read more about

Kathryn and her books at www.kathrynjane.com.

What's your recipe for a lasting, loving relationship?
One word: Compromise. You'll never both be completely happy with every decision. Pick your battles, and ask yourself, will this be important in five years? Ten? When it is important? Have a backbone and an intelligent argument.

What's the best writing advice you ever received?
Just write. Sit your butt in the chair, put your hands on the keyboard, and write, because to quote my idol, Nora Roberts, *"You can fix anything but a blank page."*

Debra H. Goldstein: Velvet Nut Chocolate Pie

1 cup slivered almonds or pecans
1 package chocolate pie filling
3/4 cup light corn syrup
3/4 cup evaporated milk
1/2 cup chocolate chips, melted
1 egg, slightly beaten
1 graham cracker crust, or crust of your choice
whipped cream

Preheat oven to 375 degrees F.

Note: If you use almonds, chop them and toast them in a 350 degree oven for 3-5 minutes. Set aside.

Blend pie filling mix, corn syrup, milk, egg, and melted chips. Pour into crust. Bake for 45 minutes or until firm and the top begins to crack.

Cool 4 hours or more. Top with the whipped cream.

Debra H. Goldstein is a retired judge whose debut novel was the 2012 IPPY award winning *Maze in Blue*. The book was also a May 2014 Harlequin Worldwide Mystery featured selection. Her recently published short stories include "Who Dat? Dat the Indian Chief!" featured in *Mardi Gras Murder*, and "Grandma's Garden," featured in *It Was a Dark and Stormy Night*. In addition, "The Rabbi's Wife Stayed Home" (Mysterical-E), "Early Frost" (Birmingham Arts Journal), "Legal Magic" (www.Alalit.com) and "A Political Cornucopia" (Bethlehem Writers Roundtable).

Debra lives in Birmingham, Alabama with her husband Joel, whose blood runs crimson. Read more about Debra at www.DebraHGoldstein.com.

What's your recipe for a lasting, loving relationship?
My life is comprised of numerous lasting, loving relationships. These relationships, which range from a thirty-plus-year marriage to friendships that pre-date meeting my husband, share one characteristic. In each, there is reciprocal love, caring and respect for the other person, but we are not blind to each other's faults.

The foundations for the various relationships differ. My marriage incorporates physical attraction, passion and compassion; my friends and I share common experiences; and, my business relationships grow from instances of admiration for professional accomplishments. No matter what the basis of the relationship, its beginning is usually rose-colored. With time, flaws appear. Rather than focusing on these annoying traits or habits, my recipe for sustaining these relationships has been to recognize and acknowledge the reality of the good and bad that exists in each person but to be willing to see less.

What's the best writing advice you ever received?
The best writing advice I ever received was to freely follow my passion but have a willingness to absorb what others can teach you. Once I accepted that writing requires discipline to get words on paper, but that it isn't a cookie cutter recipe process, I became free to explore ideas and techniques. What I learn from different individuals may be overwhelming or merely one thing, but when I adapt all of these practices into my own style, my abilities broaden and my writing improves. Sometimes, the result is a sentence that makes me believe I am a writer.

E. Ayers: Margarita Pie

Fast and easy, this is a great finish to a spicy meal.

1-1/4 cups crushed pretzels
1/2 cup butter (melted)
1/4 cup granulated sugar
2 limes, zested and juiced
1/4 cup orange juice
green food coloring (optional)
1 (14 ounce) can sweetened condensed milk
8 ounce container frozen whipped topping, thawed (or real whipped cream)
2 tablespoons Tequila (optional)
2 tablespoons Triple Sec (optional)

Place pretzels in a plastic zip bag and crush with a mallet or hammer. In a medium-size mixing bowl, combine crushed pretzels, melted butter, and sugar. Press mixture into a pie pan. Fluted pans are great. You may also use a spring-form pan, regular pie plate, or pretty dessert cups.

In a large mixing bowl, mix together lime juice, lime zest, and orange juice. Add a few drops green food coloring (if you want a greener filling) and sweetened condensed milk. Fold in whipped topping. Spoon filling into pretzel crust. Chill pie for 30 to 45 minutes.

For a more adult version drizzle Tequila and Triple Sec on top before serving.

E. Ayers is a multi-published and Amazon best-selling author of western and contemporary romances. Her books are never too sweet or too hot. She writes down the middle. She is proud to be part of the Authors of Main Street, an elite group of award-winning and best-selling contemporary authors. Read more about E. and her books at www.ayersbooks.com.

What's your recipe for a lasting, loving relationship?
Communication! It's so important to share not just the hopes and dreams,

but also the likes and dislikes, as well as the anger and frustrations of everyday life. Not every problem is fixable, but it's important to work together to achieve a harmony within the home and in the relationship. Being open, truthful and willing goes a long way. Everyone appreciates a little praise, so let your other half know you are proud of him or her.

What's the best writing advice you ever received?

Learn everything you can about the publishing industry. There's more to it than just writing the book. Things change and change quickly. As authors, we've got to be prepared because it will affect us and our readers. Whether it's where they read, on what, or how they are buying, the reader is everything to a professional author. It's important that a reader can find the author's books and enjoy the reading experience.

Chantilly White: Chocolate-Caramel Brownie Sin

Serve with ice cream for extra decadence!

18.5 ounce package chocolate cake mix
1/2 cup butter, melted
1 cup evaporated milk
10 ounce package chewy caramels. (I like to put in a few extras to make the caramel extra thick, so pick up a second bag and add a touch more evaporated milk if you're like me!)
12 ounce bag chocolate chips

Preheat oven to 350 degrees

Stir together the cake mix, butter, and 2/3 cup of the evaporated milk. Spread half the mixture into an ungreased 9" x 13" baking dish. Bake for 15 minutes. Remove from oven.

While batter is baking, heat the caramels and 1/3 cup evaporated milk in a small saucepan over low heat, stirring constantly, until the caramels are melted and smooth.

Sprinkle the chocolate chips over the baked brownie. Drizzle the caramel sauce over the chocolate chips. Drop the remaining brownie batter by spoonfuls over the caramel.

Bake for an additional 25-30 minutes, or until the center is set.

Chantilly White is a romance author who lives in the real world, but she also knows the value of escapism. As a shy girl in a scary new school, nine-year-old Chantilly discovered the priceless ability to escape her surroundings by taking pen in hand to write her own stories. Writing has been a joy ever since.

Chantilly loves providing the same joy to her readers—relaxing reads or brief escapes from their daily troubles. *Pure Hearts ~ Sinful Pleasures* is more than her tagline. It's her promise. Whether they're looking for a sweetly fluffy romantic tale or a spicy-hot romp, a sweeping historical romance or a contemporary love story, Chantilly White's readers know when they delve into one of her books, they'll be transported to a world where love reigns supreme and everyone gets their happily-ever-after. Guaranteed. Read more about Chantilly and her books at www.chantillywhite.com.

What's your recipe for a lasting, loving relationship?

As a romance writer, people often expect my key relationship ingredient to be physical attraction when it comes to recipes for romantic love. Attraction is important, of course, but without other ingredients? That would be like trying to make a delicious cake with just the frosting.

Relationships are so individual, it's tough to give a one-size-fits-all answer when it comes to creating a great recipe for lasting love, but these are my favorite ingredients—and I recommend healthy doses of each!

Humor: I'm not a naturally funny or witty person, but I don't mean comedic humor necessarily. I mean looking for and appreciating the silly stuff, keeping a positive attitude as often as possible, being willing to laugh, and remembering the importance of play.

In my family, we make time for playing together as often as possible, whether we're dressing up in our garb and attending a Renaissance Faire or a Harry Potter fan convention, watching a movie together, playing a game or a sport, whatever.

Patience: Self-explanatory, but so important. I'm not a super patient person. I'm always trying to improve, but fortunately, my husband is extra patient, which helps when he's putting up with my craziness. We've learned to balance each other's styles when it comes to handling our family life with our three children.

Thoughtfulness: Not in a gift-giving sort of way, but in a fulfilling-their-daily-needs way, even if it's just taking them a glass of ice water when they're working in the yard or doing one of their chores without being asked.

Generosity of spirit: share yourself with them, and remember they're not mind readers. Share what you need, too.

Loyalty, trust, honesty, and respect: The bedrock of any human interaction, but still crucial to note!

What's the best writing advice you ever received?

The best writing advice I've ever received is made up of three parts: write, trust your process, and finish.

When I got serious about pursuing a writing career, I stumbled around for a while before things finally clicked, thanks to the above advice and the butt-kicking capabilities of my author friends—AKA the Advice Givers.

Write: it seems obvious, but I wasted months on world-building, character creation, timelines, back-story. . . and I didn't use a bit of it. Some writers need that buildup before writing, but I'm a pantser—I write by the seat of my pants. I let everything unfold as I write, then I revise, adding or changing pertinent information as needed when the manuscript is finished.

I know that now, but it took a looooong time to figure it out and come to grips with it. I so wanted to be a plotter! I wanted graphs and storyboards and notebooks full of who-knows-what. But...

Trust your process: key word *your*. Learning craft is another issue and something that has to be done—I'm talking about your actual process of getting the story down on paper. Spend some time figuring out what it is (NOT years! A *little* time.) Accept it; use it. Run from anyone who tells you you're doing it wrong. The only right way to write is *your* way.

Finish: creative people are easily bored and most suffer from *Ooooh-Shiny Disease*. The allure of a new project is hard to ignore, but if you constantly hop on the next idea, you'll wind up with a computer full of partial manuscripts and nothing to show for all your hard work. Finish first, then reward yourself by opening that shiny new document and starting your new story.

Sloan McBride: Brownie Ice Cream Cake

19.8 ounce box brownie mix
1/2 cup vegetable oil
1/4 cup water
1/2 cup semi-sweet chocolate chips
2 eggs
Hershey's chocolate syrup (optional)
Oreos (optional)
1 quart ice cream (any flavor)
8 ounce container frozen whipped topping (I use Cool Whip.)

Preheat oven to 350 degrees F.

Combine brownie mix, vegetable oil, water and eggs in mixing bowl. Stir well with spoon until thickened and smooth (about one minute.) Spread the batter into two greased and floured 9" cake pans.

Bake until set and browned, about 30 minutes. Use toothpick to test if done. Allow to cool 10 minutes, then remove from pans and finish cooling on racks.

After brownies are cool, remove ice cream and let it soften about 10 minutes. Meanwhile, in small saucepan, melt the chocolate chips over low heat, stirring occasionally, just until chips have melted and are smooth. Remove from heat. Allow to cool until barely warm.

Place one layer of brownies into bottom of 9" spring-form pan. Evenly spread ice cream over layer. Pour half the melted chocolate chips and some Hershey's syrup (if you like really chocolately and rich) over ice cream. Place second layer of brownies on top of chocolate. Spread more ice cream, remaining melted chocolate chips and Hershey's chocolate syrup. Add a thick layer of Cool Whip on top. Optional: crush Oreos and sprinkle over Cool Whip topping. Freeze at least one hour before serving.

Sloan McBride has been a reader and writer for most of her life. In her preteens and teenage years she read Stephen King, Ken Follett and classics. In high school, she worked in the library and fed her reading addiction with an array of books about the supernatural.

Sloan currently lives in Illinois with two children, two dogs, and her husband of thirty-two years. In between her regular jobs as legal secretary, mother to two kids, wife, cook, washer-woman, chaperone, taxi driver, computer tech, and part-time creative designer for homework jobs and school projects, she writes full-length paranormal romance novels with happily-ever-after endings.

Her published works include: *Highland Stone, Together in Darkness, The Fury*, and *Dangerous Heat. The Treasure* will be released in early 2015. Read more about Sloan and her books at www.sloanmcbride.com.

What's your recipe for a lasting, loving relationship?
A lasting, loving relationship requires compromise and team work. It's plain and simple, but true. Sometimes you have to give up control and settle for what's best for the relationship. However, that doesn't mean that you have to always be the one to settle. Your partner should be willing to compromise as well. Working together toward a common goal (i.e. happily-ever-after) definitely requires teamwork. If you don't work together, it will be counterproductive, and that happily-ever-after will be out of reach.

What's the best writing advice you ever received?
I think the best writing advice I ever received was from a friend (a fellow writer) when I was struggling with writing a synopsis. She said write the synopsis as if you were sitting having coffee with a friend and telling her about the book. When I thought of it that way, the terror subsided, and my frozen fingers thawed. I was then able to put the words down on paper.

Triss Stein: Easy Crumb Cake

My mother and her mother both made this cake. I am copying it directly from the hand-written instructions my mother gave me when I moved into my first apartment.

I have no idea where it came from. It somewhat resembles a European-style kuchen, but the use of vegetable shortening gives it an American spin. The vegetable shortening instead of butter also makes it acceptable in a traditional Jewish home for serving with a meat meal. My grandmother, a Polish Jewish immigrant, kept a few recipes from a home economics class; I suspect this was one.

It is an easy cake, which freezes well and is infinitely adaptable. It can be made with any fruit suitable for pies—apple, blueberry, cherry, peach. Spice up the crust? Definitely. Try butter instead of shortening? That might be good. Add chopped nuts to crumb topping? Delicious!

Preheat oven to 425 degrees F.

2 cups flour
2/3 cup shortening
4 tablespoons sugar (or less to taste)
pinch of salt
1 egg, lightly beaten
your favorite fruit pie filling or fresh fruit

Mix dry ingredients together. Cut shortening into flour as you would for pie crust. Blend egg into mixture. Reserve about 1/3 cup of crumbs. Pat the rest into the bottom and up the sides to the top edge of an 8" x 8" pan.

Pour fruit filling into pan. Sprinkle reserved crumbs on top. Bake about 35-40 minutes or until top is golden.

Note: If using an 8" x 13" pan, increase flour to 3 cups, shortening to 1 cup, and sugar to 6 tablespoons.

Triss Stein is a small town girl from New York dairy country who has spent most of her adult life living and working in New York City. This gives her the double vision of both a stranger and a resident for writing mysteries about Brooklyn, her ever-fascinating, ever-challenging adopted home. She's inspired by its varied neighborhoods and their rich histories, as is her heroine Erica, an urban historian-in-training and single mother of a teenaged daughter. Her research sometimes leads her to dangerous questions and crimes that are not historical.

In *Brooklyn Bones*, it's a body, hidden behind a wall in her own home in gentrifying Park Slope. *Brooklyn Graves* is about historic Green-Wood Cemetery, Tiffany glass, a turn-of-the-last century mystery, and some up-to-date crimes. Her book in progress will be about Brooklyn gangs past and present. Read more about Triss and her books at www.trissstein.com.

What's your recipe for a lasting, loving relationship?
I was fortunate to grow up in a home where my parents really loved each other. They argued, of course, and became exasperated at times, but no one who knew them ever doubted that they had the real thing: affection, respect, trust.

They married young, had three children in four years, had many years when money was short and the future didn't seem very certain, but they were optimistic people in an optimistic era. Their marriage lasted almost sixty-five years. It took my mother a long time to believe my dad was really gone.

So, when my father spoke about marriage, you can be sure I paid attention. He told me, "People say marriage is a 50/50 proposition but that's wrong. It's when both partners are giving 60% that it adds up just right."

Does that sound too easy? Simplistic? It calls for deep emotional generosity and the trust that it will be returned. I've tried to hold it in my heart all these years. I passed it to one daughter and son-in-law as part of a wedding toast and will soon do it again for my other daughter. He was a wise old man, Grandpa Simon.

What's the best writing advice you ever received?

My favorite piece of writing advice has been attributed to at least three authors. William Faulkner appears to be the leading contender. There's a lot to be said for stealing wisdom from the best: *"I only write when I am inspired. Fortunately I get inspired at 9:00 every morning."* That says it all about the crucial difference between "someone who writes" and "a writer."

My other favorite is a comfort to me, a non-outliner, when I am lost in the dark and the fog, with no idea what happens next. The great E.L. Doctorow said, *"Writing a book is like driving a car at night. You never see further than your headlights, but you can make the whole trip that way."*

These are my two mantras, but for a longer piece of advice, you cannot do better than Stephen King's "Everything You Need to Know About Writing Successfully—in Ten Minutes." (You can find it online by doing a Google search.)

Debra Holland: Strawberry Pretzel Dessert

1-1/2 cups salted pretzels, crushed
1 cup sugar
1/2 cup butter, melted
9 ounces Cool Whip, thawed
8 ounces cream cheese
2 packages (3 ounces each) strawberry Jell-O
2 packages (10 ounces each) frozen strawberries, partially thawed
2 cups boiling water

Preheat oven to 350 degrees F.

Mix pretzels with butter and 1/2 cup sugar. Pat into a 9"x13" pan. Bake for 10 minutes.

Blend cream cheese and 1/2 cup sugar. Fold in Cool Whip. Spread over pretzel crust. Place in refrigerator to cool.

Dissolve Jell-O with the 2 cups boiling water. Add partially thawed strawberries. Place in refrigerator to thicken slightly. Once slightly thickened, spread over cream cheese mixture.
Let set overnight. Cut into squares to serve.

Debra Holland is a *New York Times* and *USA Today* bestselling author. She also holds a Ph.D and is a psychotherapist and marriage counselor, so she knows about relationships. She's the author of the award-winning sweet historical Western romance Montana Sky series, as well as fantasy romance The Gods' Dream Trilogy and the romantic space opera Twinborne Trilogy.

Debra is also the author of the non-fiction book, *The Essential Guide to Grief and Grieving* from Alpha Books (a subsidiary of Penguin) and is a contributing author to *The Naked Truth About Self-Publishing*. *58 Tips for Getting What You Want From a Difficult Conversation* is a free e-booklet that can be found on her website. Read more about Debra and her books at www.drdebraholland.com.

What's your recipe for a lasting, loving relationship?
Continue to treat each other in the same way you did when you were courting—loving, respectful, communicative, forgiving, and romantic.

What's the best writing advice you ever received?
Don't give up writing, no matter what the setbacks!

Ana Morgan: Pumpkin Pie Squares

1 cup flour
1/2 cup quick oats
1/2 cup brown sugar
1/2 cup butter plus 2 tablespoons
2 cups pumpkin puree
1 can evaporated milk
2 eggs
1-1/4 cups sugar
1/2 teaspoon salt
1 teaspoon cinnamon
1/2 teaspoon ginger
1/4 teaspoon cloves
1/2 cup chopped pecans
1/2 cup sugar
2 tablespoons butter

Preheat oven to 350 degrees F.

To make crust, blend flour, oats, brown sugar, and 1/2 cup butter until crumbly. Press into 9" x 13" pan. Bake for 15 minutes.

Combine pumpkin puree, evaporated milk, eggs, 3/4 cup sugar, salt, cinnamon, ginger, and cloves. Mix well.

Remove crust from oven and pour filling over crust. Return to oven and bake for 20 minutes more.

Combine chopped pecans, 1/2 cup sugar, and 2 tablespoons butter. Sprinkle over pumpkin filling. Return pan to oven and cook for another 15-20 minutes.

Cool and serve with whipped cream.

Ana Morgan lives in a log cabin on a farm nestled in Minnesota's north woods. She pays the bills by managing her specialty food business. Ana has been a newspaper and magazine gardening columnist and contributed articles to various national magazines. Her poems and creative non-fiction have appeared in the Jackpine Writers Guild annual anthology.

Ana has four practically perfect grandchildren and a husband who served in Vietnam. Read more about Ana at www.heroineswithhearts.blogspot.com.

What's your recipe for a lasting, loving relationship?

Truthfully, a relationship with a PTSD sufferer is challenging. I've been married for forty-five years, and I'm still discovering joys and solutions. My ingredients include Patience. Forgiveness. Great sex. Being willing to admit you are wrong when you are wrong, and saying, "I'm sorry." Signing on for things that don't allow for an easy out when you hit a rough patch, like children or a mortgage. Remembering that life is constantly changing and evolving. Nothing stays the same.

What's the best writing advice you ever received?

Don't publish until you are sure you've written the best book you can. Then let it fly, and start the next one.

Adele Downs: Retro Homemade Peach Pie

Use ripe organic peaches, real butter, and as many other organic ingredients as possible for the best-tasting, old-fashioned double-crust pie you've ever eaten. Serves 8.

15 ounce package pastry for a 9" double-crust pie.
1 egg, beaten
5 cups peaches, peeled and sliced
2 tablespoons fresh-squeezed lemon juice
1/4 tablespoon vanilla extract
1/4 cup all-purpose flour
1/4 cup corn starch
1/2 cup white sugar
1/2 cup brown sugar
1/2 teaspoon ground cinnamon
1/4 teaspoon ground ginger
1/4 teaspoon salt
2 tablespoons butter (don't use margarine)
vanilla ice cream (optional)

Preheat oven to 450 degrees F. (For best results, preheat the oven with a pizza stone inside and bake the pie on top of the pizza stone. If a pizza stone isn't available, use center oven rack.)

Line 9" pie plate with one of the pie crusts. Brush with beaten egg to keep the crust firm.

Place sliced peaches, vanilla extract, and lemon juice in a large bowl. Toss gently to coat peaches.

In separate bowl, mix flour, cornstarch, sugars, cinnamon, ginger, and salt. Transfer the mixture to the bowl of peaches and toss gently. Pour ingredients into the pie crust. Dot with butter.
Cover the pie with the second crust, folding edges under. Flute the edges or

use the tines of a fork dipped in egg to seal them. Brush the remaining egg over the top crust. Cut at least four slits in the top crust to release steam while baking.

Bake for 10 minutes. Reduce heat to 350 degrees F and bake an additional 30-35 minutes until crust is brown and the juice bubbles through the vents. To prevent the edges from browning too quickly, cover them with strips of aluminum foil about halfway through baking time, or use aluminum pie crust ring. Cool before serving.

Adele Downs writes contemporary romance novels, some with a touch of magic, inside the office of her rural Pennsylvania home. She's a former journalist, published in newspapers and magazines inside the USA, UK, and Caribbean. Adele is an active member of Romance Writers of America and her local RWA chapter where she serves as a past-president. She has written several articles for RWR magazine (Romance Writers Report) and has presented workshops for writers. Her titles include *Kissing Her Cowboy*, *Naturally Yours*, *Her Christmas Cowboy*, *Her Immortal Viking*, *Santa To The Rescue*, as well as several others.

When Adele isn't working on her current project, she can be found riding in her convertible or reading a book on the nearest beach. Read more about Adele and her books at www.adeledowns.wordpress.com.

What's your recipe for a loving, lasting relationship?
My husband and I consider mutual respect the primary ingredient for a happy marriage. When a relationship is based on respect, all the other ingredients for a satisfying relationship follow. We put consideration for one another above everything else. After twenty-eight years together, we're convinced our recipe is the secret to marital harmony and long-lasting love.

What's the best writing advice you ever received?
The only way to break through writer's block is to write your way through it. Keep going and the ideas will flow again.

L.C. Giroux: Marquise au Chocolat

3/4 pound semisweet chocolate or a mix of semisweet and dark chocolate
3/4 cup butter
1/2 cup superfine (caster) sugar
4 eggs, separated
1 teaspoon peppermint or orange flavoring (optional)

Note: This recipe will take 30 minutes (or less) to make plus overnight chilling.

Break up chocolate and place in a microwave-safe bowl. Microwave for one minute, stir, microwave again for 30-45 seconds and stir again. Repeat until chocolate is melted.

Cream butter and sugar, then add the melted chocolate and mix well. Add the egg yolks one at a time, mixing well after each. Add optional flavor.

Whip the egg whites until very stiff. Fold the egg whites into the chocolate mixture with a wooden spoon until just mixed. You don't want to take the air out of them, but if you overdo it the cake will still be delicious, just not as tall and light.

Pour batter into an oiled spring-form pan or a loaf pan lined with plastic wrap or parchment. Press down (I cover the top with plastic wrap) to remove any big air bubbles. Chill for 12 hours.

Technically, this keeps in the refrigerator for several days. I say *technically* because...well, you try not eating it all sooner. Oh, and no, you didn't read the recipe wrong. There is no actual baking with this recipe. I've made this dozens of times and never had anyone become ill.

L.C. Giroux is a bestselling author who writes smart, sexy, fun, contemporary and new adult romance novels. She's written more than twelve books that are as much about the love of a family as about any one couple.

Romance might be an odd fit after an architecture degree and careers in cosmetics and molecular biology, but five minutes into their first date she knew she had met her future husband. Twenty years later, one kid, and their fair share of richer, poorer, sickness, and health, and she still believes in a happy ending.

Her latest book is *This Day Forward*, the last book in her Lovers and Other Strangers series. Read more about L.C. and her books at www.lcgiroux.com.

What's your recipe for a lasting, loving relationship?
Remember your teacher or grandmother telling you that you had two ears and only one mouth for a reason? Still good advice but I would add that just listening with your ears isn't enough. You need to hear with your heart, too. Listening without thinking about what you are going to say next is hard. Opening your heart to hear what the other person is really saying is even harder, but if you can do it, all of your relationships get better.

What's the best writing advice you ever received?
Finish the draft! If you don't get the basic ideas down on the page (or on the screen,) you can't move forward. You can't edit, have other people read it, sell it, make other people feel things they wouldn't without your words. It doesn't have to be perfect; heck it doesn't even have to be good the first time. But without that first draft there are just voices chattering in your head, and I'm pretty sure you need medication for that.

Diana Orgain: No-Bake Peanut Butter, Marshmallow, Chocolate, Oatmeal Cookies

1-3/4 cups sugar
1/2 cup milk
4 tablespoons unsweetened cocoa powder
1/4 cup (1/2 stick) unsalted butter
3 cups quick cook oatmeal
1 cup peanut butter
1 teaspoon vanilla extract
1 cup mini marshmallows

In a large, heavy-bottomed saucepan, add the sugar, milk, and butter, stirring to combine. Cook over high heat and bring to a boil. Allow to boil for 1 minute.

In a separate bowl, mix together oats, peanut butter, and marshmallows. Add the sugar mixture to the bowl, then the vanilla extract. Stir well to combine.

Drop by tablespoonfuls onto waxed paper-lined cookie sheet. Chill.

Diana Orgain is the bestselling author of the Maternal Instincts Mystery Series: *Bundle of Trouble, Motherhood is Murder, Formula for Murder*, and *Nursing a Grudge*. She is the co-author of *Gilt Trip* in the *New York Times* bestselling Scrapbooking Mystery Series by Laura Childs. *A First Date with Death*, the first in her Love or Money Mystery series, will be published by Penguin in spring 2015. *Yappy Hour*, the first in a new Roundup Crew Mystery series, will be published by St. Martin in fall 2015.

Diana lives in San Francisco with her husband and three children. Read more about Diana and her books at www.dianaorgain.com.

What's your recipe for a lasting, loving relationship?
Listen! And my favorite is the Golden Rule: treat others how you want to be

treated!

What's the best writing advice you ever received?

Storytelling is about emotion. Plot is about what happens to your characters, yes, but more importantly how they *feel* about what is happening to them. One of my first writing teachers told me that if the author didn't laugh or cry at her manuscript, then the reader wouldn't either. Bottom line is you have to *feel* your story before your characters or readers will.

Pamela Aares: Home Run Shortbread Almond Cookies

Who says vegan and wheat free desserts can't be delicious? These delightful, crunchy cookies are perfect with a cup of spiced tea or lemonade!

1 cup roasted almonds
3/4 cup rolled oats
1/2 cup canola, sunflower or safflower oil
1/2 cup maple syrup
1-1/2 teaspoons vanilla extract
1/2 teaspoon almond extract (optional)
1/2 cup amaranth flour
1/2 cup rice flour
1/2 teaspoon baking soda
1/2 teaspoon baking powder
1/2 teaspoon salt
2 teaspoons cinnamon

Preheat oven to 350 degrees F.

Process almond and oat flour in food processor to consistency of coarse flour. Transfer to a large bowl and set aside.

In a smaller bowl stir together the maple syrup, vanilla extract, optional almond extract, and oil.

Sift the remaining dry ingredients into the almond and oat mixture. Pour the wet ingredients into the dry ingredients and stir until well mixed.

Using two spoons, scoop out cookie mixture onto well greased or parchment lined baking sheets. Using an oiled finger or a glass (dip in warm water to prevent sticking,) flatten each cookie. They should be about bite size.

Bake for 11 minutes. Turn baking sheets at 5 minutes and check cookies at around 10 minutes. Cookies should be a golden brown. Cool on sheets for 5 minutes, then remove cookies to a cooling rack. Store in an airtight container.

Pamela Aares is an award-winning, internationally bestselling author of contemporary and historical romance novels (*Jane Austen and the Archangel.*) Her latest books, the Tavonesi series (*Love Bats Last, Thrown By Love, Fielder's Choice, Love on the Line*, and *Aim for Love,*) are about romance in sports and feature alpha male All-Stars and the strong women they come to love. Her popularity as a romance author continues to grow with each new book release, so much so, that the Bay area author has drawn comparisons by readers and reviewers to Nora Roberts.

Before becoming a romance author, Pamela wrote and produced award-winning films including *Your Water, Your Life*, featuring actress Susan Sarandon and the NPR series *New Voices, The Powers of the Universe* and *The Earth's Imagination*. She holds a Master's degree from Harvard and currently resides in the wine country of Northern California with her husband, a former MLB All-Star, and two curious cats.

If not behind her computer, you can probably find Pamela reading a romance novel, hiking the beach, or savoring life with friends. Read more about Pamela and her books at www.PamelaAares.com.

What's your recipe for a lasting, loving relationship?
Stay in touch with the miracle of the other person and the preciousness of life. If you see your beloved with fresh eyes every day, no matter what, your love will flourish. Remember the little things: please, thank you, you're welcome. Treat conversations as opportunities to cherish and deepen your love, no matter how tough the subject matter!

What's the best writing advice you ever received?
Write, write, write!

Nancy Warren: Maids of Honour

My parents are British, so English baking was a tradition in our house when I was growing up. My mother was and is an excellent cook as was her mother before her. This recipe is my grandmother's. It's called Maids of Honour. The recipe apparently originated at Hampton Court. The story is that Henry VIII stumbled upon Anne Boleyn and her ladies in waiting eating these delicious tarts, tried one, and promptly proclaimed these "Maids of Honour" to be delicious. The originals contained mashed potato and cheese curd. My grandmother's recipe is much nicer, I think.

I still associate the smell of baking almond tarts with good things like birthdays, or even coming in after school on a cold, rainy day and finding hot tea and fresh baking. I've continued the tradition and often bake these for my family.

pastry dough (your own recipe or frozen)
raspberry jam
2 tablespoons butter
1 cup sugar
1 egg, beaten
1 cup ground almonds
1/4 teaspoon almond extract
sliced almonds (optional)

Preheat oven to 400 degrees F.

Make your usual pastry dough recipe or defrost frozen dough. Roll out and cut with fluted cookie cutter into twelve tart shells. Place in tart pans.

Place a small amount of raspberry jam in the bottom of each tart shell.

Cream butter, gradually add sugar, beating between additions. Stir in beaten egg, nuts and almond extract. Place a spoonful of mixture into each tart shell. Add a sprinkle of sliced almonds over the top.
Bake approximately 20 minutes or until set. Cool before serving.

Nancy Warren is the *USA Today* bestselling author of more than fifty novels. She's known for writing funny, sexy and suspenseful tales. She calls Vancouver, Canada home, though she tends to wander. She's an avid hiker, animal lover, wine drinker and chocolate fiend.

Favorite moments in her career include being featured on the front page of the *New York Times* when she launched Harlequin's NASCAR series with *Speed Dating*. She was also the answer to a crossword puzzle clue in Canada's *National Post* newspaper. She's been a double-finalist in the RITA awards and has won the Reviewer's Choice Award from *Romantic Times* magazine.

Nancy is the author of the best selling Toni Diamond Mystery Series and the Take a Chance romance series, among others. Learn more about Nancy and her books at www.nancywarren.net.

What's your recipe for a lasting, loving relationship?

As a romance author, I not only enjoy some very good long term relationships, but I spend a lot of time watching happy couples. You know the ones who post gushing tributes to their spouse on Facebook after five or ten or thirty years of marriage. I think the secret recipe to any lasting love, whether a friend or a spouse, is to focus on the positive.

I have a friend who is always late. Always. I got to the point where I almost ended our friendship, but then I thought about all the things I love about her and that we've been friends since high school. Now, when we arrange to meet, I always take a book with me and plan to spend time reading while I wait. I love that unexpected fifteen or twenty minutes with a good book. It was such a simple fix. I think with a romance it's the same. Even when your partner is at his or her most irritating, focus on the things you love about him or her. It's a lot easier than trying to get them to change!

What's the best writing advice you ever received?

This came from Susan Elizabeth Phillips (who is one of my favourite authors of all time.) She said, *"Protect the work."* I have taken this to mean that the first draft is between me and my muse. I try not to talk about the book I'm working on, or to share too much until I have a solid first draft. You can and should listen to editors and reviewers and readers, but good books don't get written by committees. The gift of creativity is a precious one. We need to honour it.

And now, if you'll excuse me, I think I will bake a batch of Maids of Honour for my beloved muse.

Barbara Lohr: Sunshine Cake

This light cake is only about 1-1/2" tall. Perfect for a summer day!

1 cup flour
2 teaspoons baking powder
1/4 teaspoon salt
1 stick unsalted butter, softened
3/4 cup sugar plus 1/2 tablespoon
2 eggs
1 teaspoon vanilla extract
2 peaches, pitted and sliced (other fruits also work well)
1 teaspoon nutmeg

Preheat over to 350 degrees F.

Whisk together flour, baking powder and salt.

Beat butter and 3/4 cup sugar with electric mixer until pale and fluffy. Add eggs one at a time, beating well after each addition. Then beat in extract. Mix in flour mixture at low speed.

Drop large clumps of batter into lightly buttered spring-form pan and spread evenly. Scatter peach slices on top of batter.

Stir nutmeg into 1/2 tablespoon sugar. Sprinkle over top. Bake about 45-50 minutes until cake is golden brown and top springs back when touched. Cool fifteen minutes. Remove side of pan and cool.

Barbara Lohr writes contemporary romance, adult as well as new adult, often with a humorous twist. Early in her career she taught writing and literature, providing a springboard for her later work in advertising and marketing. Literature remained her passion, both writing and reading. In her novels feisty women take on hunky heroes and life's issues. Windy City Romance, her first series (*Her Favorite Mistake*, *Her Favorite Honeymoon*, and *Her Favorite Hot*

Doc) presents resilient women, who were high school friends, and the men they love. Her novellas include *Summer of the Fireflies*, *Summer Riptide* and *The Salty Carmel Christmas*.

Barbara lives in the Midwest with her husband and their cat, who claims he was Heathcliff in another life. In addition to travel, her interests include golf and cooking. She makes a mean popover. Read more about Barbara and her books at www.BarbaraLohrAuthor.com.

What's your recipe for a lasting, loving relationship?
Long lasting relationships are based on respect and patience.

What's the best writing advice you ever received?
Put butt in chair and write!

J.J. Cook: Hot Pepper Corn Muffins

From Playing With Fire, *A Sweet Pepper Fire Brigade Mystery. Recipe makes 1-dozen muffins.*

2 cups of self-rising, yellow corn meal
1 cup self-rising flour (If you don't have self-rising, add 1 teaspoon of baking powder)
2 eggs
1 cup milk
1/4 cup cooking oil
1 tablespoon sugar or sweetener
4 jalapenos, chopped, seeded and stems removed or hotter peppers per your taste

Preheat oven to 350 degrees F.

For the basic muffin batter mix together the cornmeal, flours, eggs, milk, cooking oil, and sugar.

Add peppers. A mixture of red and green peppers creates a festive look!

Coat a muffin tin with cooking spray. Fill each space. Bake for 20 minutes or until a toothpick comes out clean.

J. J. Cook writes award-winning, bestselling mystery fiction as themselves, Joyce and Jim Lavene, and as Ellie Grant. They have written and published more than 70 novels for Harlequin, Penguin, Amazon, and Simon and Schuster, along with hundreds of non-fiction articles for national and regional publications. They live in rural North Carolina with their family. Read more about them and their books at www.joyceandjimlavene.com.

What's your recipe for a lasting, loving relationship?
Mix two parts love and two parts friendship with two parts understanding and enjoying the same things in life with a heaping handful of getting through

hard times with our faith intact, and voila! That is my recipe for a long relationship.

What's the best writing advice you ever received?
"Write every day no matter what. Go to bed late. Get up early. Let something go. Don't let a day pass by without writing something to work toward your goal of being published."— Author Janet Dailey

Lynn Reynolds: Lemon Victory Cake

This recipe is both dairy and egg-free.

Sometimes this is called Depression Cake, but my mom preferred to call it Victory Cake, after the Victory Gardens popular in World War II.

In the Great Depression, and later in World War II, lots of foods were costly or in short supply. Many basics were rationed. It was a rare treat to get milk, butter or eggs, so creative cooks came up with recipes that avoided these ingredients. My mother had an entire cookbook sent out by the local utility company during WWII that adapted many recipes with these new restrictions in mind. She took those recipes and tweaked them over the years, then passed her revised recipes on to me. When my son was diagnosed with a milk allergy and I was diagnosed with an egg allergy, I found a whole new use for those old WWII recipes.

2 cups of sugar
2/3 cup of vegetable oil (I use canola. Avoid oils that have a strong flavor of their own, like olive oil – unless you *want* an olive-flavored cake!)
3 cups of all-purpose unbleached flour
1 teaspoon of salt
2 teaspoons of baking soda
2 tablespoons of lemon juice (or white vinegar)
1-1/2 - 2 cups of water (or almond milk)
1 teaspoon vanilla extract (optional)
1 stick Earth Balance vegan margarine or Fleischmann's Unsalted Margarine
1-1/2 cups 10x confectioner's sugar
1-2 tablespoons lemon juice or cold water
2 squares semi-sweet dark chocolate (optional)

Preheat oven to 350 degrees F.

Note: For vanilla cake, use white vinegar instead of lemon juice and include the vanilla extract.
Blend sugar and oil until smooth. Blend in the flour and salt by hand or on

low speed.

Mix the baking soda and lemon juice (or vinegar) together. Add the mixture to the cake batter. Add the water (or almond milk) and blend on low speed until smooth.

Pour into greased and floured 9" x 13" cake pan and bake for about 35 minutes. Test the center with a toothpick to make sure the dough is baked all the way through. Cool the cake, then frost. Or for a quick snack cake, just dust the top with confectioner's sugar.

To make the dairy-free "Victory" frosting, mix the margarine, confectioner's sugar, and 1-2 tablespoons lemon juice or cold water on high-speed until creamy. Be sure to add the lemon juice or water very gradually so the frosting doesn't get runny. If it does, just add a little more confectioner's sugar to thicken it up again.

For chocolate frosting on a vanilla cake, use the water instead of lemon juice. Melt a couple of squares of semi-sweet dark chocolate and add to the frosting mix. Spread on a completely cooled cake.

Lynn Reynolds is a city girl, forever trapped in Green Acres, who writes mysteries, suspense, and contemporary romance. *RT Book Reviews* called her debut chick noir novel *Thirty-Nine Again "a first-class mystery...and a first-class read."* A new chick noir novel will be released in 2015. (Lynn claims chick noir is a lot like chick lit, only with guns and dead bodies instead of shoes.)

Lynn's cakes, cobblers, and blueberry pie are lauded by family members far and wide. She has been meaning to write a cookbook for years and is thrilled to be included in *Bake, Love, Write*. Read more about Lynn and her books at www.lynnreynolds.com.

What's your recipe for a lasting, loving relationship?
1 sympathetic ear—ready to listen and not judge
1 cup of patience, so the other person's little quirks don't make you crazy

A great big pinch of humor, to better enjoy the good times and to make the bad times bearable

Stir together generously. Serve as often as desired.

What's the best writing advice you ever received?

The world is so full of writing advice, isn't it? Write first thing in the morning; write late at night. Write every day; write only when you feel inspired. Write in a café where there's noise and activity; write in a library where it's quiet and calm. You should write what you know; you should write the story you'd like to read. You should write about strange new worlds. Some will say you should never write in the first person; others tell you personal is better. Write long; write short. Use lots of adverbs; adverbs are evil! Use lots of description; leave the descriptions up to the reader's imagination. And of course, always remember: Show, don't tell!

It's enough to give an aspiring author a migraine.

The best advice I've ever heard about writing is from my mother, who was not a writer but knew that I wanted to be one. "Write what you love," she said, "and the money will follow. Or it won't. But at least you'll have written something you love."

And the second best bit of advice comes from bestselling author Joseph Finder (although it's been said by many authors in many different ways): *Just finish the damned book already.* In other words, stop polishing that perfect first chapter and get to the sloppy, messy ending. Otherwise, you have nothing.

Cori Lynn Arnold: "Some Like it Hot" Brownies

I am not a gardener, per se, but every summer I do my best to keep up with my mother-in-law's garden harvest. We chop, pickle, jam, salsa, and grill every fruit and vegetable we pick. Nothing goes to waste. But this summer, my mother-in-law accidentally bought seventy-two pepper plants, most of them hot pepper plants. I've had to get a little creative with using those peppers, so this piquant brownie recipe was born.

1/2 cup butter
1-1/4 cups sugar
2 eggs
1 habanero and 1 jalapeno (extra spicy) or 2 jalapenos (medium) or 1 jalapeno (mild) finely chopped (I recommend a food processor)
1/3 cup unsweetened cocoa powder
1/2 cup bread flour
1/4 teaspoon salt
1/4 teaspoon baking powder

Preheat oven to 350 degrees F.

Melt butter in microwave. In large bowl mix together melted butter, sugar, eggs and finely chopped peppers. Beat in cocoa, flour, salt and baking powder. Spread into greased and floured 7" x 11" brownie pan.

Bake for 25-30 minutes. To prevent brownie dryness, do not overcook.

Cori Lynn Arnold is the author of the novel *Scalding Deceit*. She has worked as a hotel housekeeper, handy woman, laundry attendant, radio disc jockey, library clerk, historical photographic archivist, mathematics tutor, teaching assistant, art work framer, photo lab junky, portrait and wedding photographer, high school algebra teacher, internet security researcher, security analyst, computer programmer and ethical hacker. She currently resides in Connecticut and can be found roaming from coffee shops to bookstores wearing the same cheap "good luck" sweater ripping apart at the seams. Cori doesn't have a website, but you can learn more about her and her writing on Facebook.

What's your recipe for a lasting, loving relationship?
My grandmother had four kids, including my mother. She never let any of them get between her and her husband. She is happily enjoying a sixty-five year marriage. She always says that kids are great, they are a joy to your life, but your spouse comes first.

What's the best writing advice you ever received?
Write it bad; just write it down.

B.V. Lawson: Espresso Brownies

My main protagonist, Scott Drayco, is a bachelor who swears he "burns water" when he tries to cook, but even he can manage this simple recipe.

1 box fudge brownie mix
1 bottle Manhattan Special Espresso Soda (or other 10-ounce espresso soda)

Preheat oven to 350 degrees F.

Dump the brownie mix into a large mixing bowl. Slowly pour the espresso soda over the dry brownie mix, and stir together with a spatula, whisk or mixer. The batter may appear thin.

Spray the bottom of a 9" x 13" pan with cooking spray. Pour batter into pan and bake as directed on the box until a toothpick inserted in the center comes out clean. (You may need to add 5-10 minutes to baking time.) Cool before cutting into squares.

B.V. Lawson is an award-winning author and journalist whose stories, poems and articles have appeared in dozens of national and regional publications and anthologies. A three-time Derringer Award finalist and 2012 winner for her short fiction, B.V. was also honored by the American Independent Writers and Maryland Writers Association for her Scott Drayco series.

B.V. currently lives in Virginia with her husband and enjoys flying above the Chesapeake Bay in a little Cessna. Read more about B.V. and her books at www.bvlawson.com. No ticket required.

What's your recipe for a lasting, loving relationship?

Respect + trust + empathy + forgiveness. Respect is the bond that holds relationships together, trust is the leavening that arises from respecting your partner, and empathy is the tenderizer. Forgiveness is needed for the occasional mess we all create from time to time.

What's the best writing advice you ever received?

"When I feel that surge of excitement, I know I've hit upon the right idea for a scene...If you're trusting your gut reaction to what you're writing (i.e., trusting your body and not listening to the committee in your mind), you'll do fine." – Elizabeth George

Lynn Franklin: The Comfort Apple Pie

Apple pie tips:
1. The best pies taste both sweet and tart with an underlying spiciness. Choose a mixture of sweet, tart and aromatic apples such as Granny Smith, Gala, and Golden Delicious.

2. Sample the apples. Apples sweeten in storage. If your tart apples aren't tart enough, add a little lemon juice to the apple mixture.

3. For a chunky pie, slice apples by hand.

4. For best results, prepare filling and topping before rolling out the crust.

4 Granny Smith apples, peeled, cored and sliced
4 Gala apples, peeled, cored and sliced
4 Golden Delicious apples, peeled, cored and sliced
1/3 cup sugar
1 tablespoon cinnamon
1/4 teaspoon lemon juice (optional, see above)
1 Prepared 10" pie crust
1 cup flour
1 cup brown sugar
1/4 teaspoon salt
1/2 cup butter, softened
1/4 teaspoon vanilla extract

Preheat oven to 325 degrees F.

Peel, core and slice apples. Add sugar and cinnamon. Mix well. Set aside while you prepare topping.

In large bowl, mix flour, brown sugar and salt. With pastry blender, cut butter into mixture until crumbly. Add vanilla extract and mix.

Roll out pie crust and place in pie plate; form decorative edges. Pour apples into crust. Make sure you include the cinnamon/sugar syrup that developed while you were preparing the pie crust. Apples will mound up high above the pie plate (They will cook down to fill plate.)

Gently press topping onto apples, making sure apples are completely covered. Place cookie sheet on rack beneath pie to catch drippings. Bake approximately 1 hour and 20 minutes until apples are soft (insert paring knife in center to test) and crust is golden.

Lynn Franklin often accompanied her jeweler grandfather on his local buying trips when she was a child. As they traipsed the grungy streets of Pittsburgh, Grandpa carried a battered briefcase filled with diamonds, emeralds, rubies and sapphires. These trips provided fertile ground for Lynn's imagination, allowing her to search the shadows for thugs, thieves and spies.

So it came as no surprise when at the age of eight, she demanded a deerstalker hat and wrote her first mystery novel. To hone her sleuthing skills, she studied the case files of Nancy Drew, Frank and Joe Hardy, and Trixie Belden.

In time, Lynn became a professional writer, an Accredited Jewelry Professional and the author of Amazon's acclaimed Jeweler's Gemstone Mystery series. In *The Pirate's Ruby*, geologist/psychology professor Kimberley West must follow an ancient ruby's trail of death to save a child from a jewel thief who's not afraid to kill. Read more about Lynn and her books at www.LynnFranklin.com.

What's your recipe for a lasting, loving relationship?
My advice is for keeping harmony in a large, extended family. To do so, thoroughly combine 2 cups patience, 1 cup sense of humor, 1/2 cup trust, and 1 tablespoon of a taste for adventure.

And always remember: As frustrating as family members can seem, they do love you—and they haven't told your new beau about the time you hid in the apple tree and tried to convince the neighbors they'd been invaded by howler monkeys.

What's the best writing advice you ever received?

My first-grade teacher warned my parents that I'd grow up to be a writer (Mom promptly asked, "How will you earn a living?") Given my early and continual exposure to the writing world, I can confidently say I've heard every crazy piece of advice ever given to new writers. *You must find your voice!* (Huh?) *Write what you know about!* (But what if I want to write a murder mystery?) *You can only be a writer if you love words!* (Isn't that like saying an artist must love paintbrushes?)

If you, too, have been bitten by the writing bug and are confused by the mountain of advice floating around universities, writing workshops, and the Internet, fear not. Everyone's advice can be boiled down into one sentence: Focus on clarity.

Too many of us try to out-Shakespeare Shakespeare. We insert beautiful words, lovely metaphors and deep symbolism. Then we wonder why our readers' eyes glaze over.

Try this instead: After you've created your characters and developed your plot, write the story as if you're leading your reader from one thought to another without making them stumble. Ask your first readers to flag any place where they became confused, then rewrite those sections. After rewriting, ask your next editors to also note places where they stumbled. And rewrite again.

Keep the question, "Is this clear?" in your mind. Then sit back and enjoy your readers as they gobble up your work and talk about your "fast pace" and "fun, easy writing style."

M.L. Guida: Pizzeles

Pizzeles are Italian cookies made with a pizzele iron. This recipe came from my great-grandmother from Italy and is a family favorite. Orange peel can be shredded to give it an extra zest. The best part to making pizzeles is the fragrant scent. It will fill your house with Christmas. Inhale and enjoy.

1 pound margarine (Don't use butter; it will burn.)
15 eggs
2-1/2 cups sugar
1 bottle anise oil (flavoring is too weak)
5-6 cups unsifted flour

Melt margarine. Allow to cool.

Beat eggs. Stir in sugar, then anise oil, then cooled margarine. Add flour. Mix all together. Let set half an hour before using pizzele iron.

M.L. Guida loves the paranormal. At four years of age she watched *Dark Shadows* and fell in love with vampires. Who wouldn't want a bite on the neck? Currently, she has two series with vampires: the Legends of the Soaring Phoenix and Vampires on Holiday. Today, she continues to love the preternatural and has ventured into more supernatural beings, specifically demons, but not just any demons—dragon demons. Her newest series is The Underworld.

M.L. lives in Colorado near the Rocky Mountains. She loves to take her cocker spaniel Sadie for walks on the trails behind her house. When she travels, she tries to go on ghost tours. Her favorite so far was the Jack the Ripper tour in London.

M.L. currently writes for Kensington/Lyrical Imprint, Passion in Print, and self-publishes. She is a member of Colorado Romance Writers and Romance Writers of America. Read more about M.L. at www.mlguida.com.

What's your recipe for a lasting relationship?
My recipe is laughter. Life is hard, and laughter makes even the toughest times lighter. With my current friends, family, and past love relationships, laughing has helped ease the problems of this world. I like developing secret code words with friends or boyfriends that make me smile, watching comedies together, and just enjoying life. A sense of humor is key in a relationship; without it, there's no sparkle.

What's the best writing advice you ever received?
My best advice on writing is for writers to have perseverance. This is a tough business with rejections and once published, reviews. I learned to evaluate my rejections, and then enrolled in craft classes to work on my craft. I also have a critique partner who assesses my strengths and weaknesses. I find her invaluable. If you plan to self-publish, then you need a quality cover and a good editor. But the most important rule is to never give up!

Irene Peterson: Simple Tasty Cake

1-1/3 cups sifted all-purpose flour
3/4 cup sugar
2 teaspoons baking powder
1/2 teaspoon salt
1/4 cup shortening or margarine
2/3 cup milk
1 egg
1 teaspoon vanilla extract
8 ounce package cream cheese, softened
1 jar Marshmallow Fluff
1 teaspoon maraschino cherry juice
chopped fruit (optional)

Preheat oven to 350 F.

Note: Double recipe to make a layer cake.

Sift flour, sugar, baking powder, and salt into large mixing bowl. Add shortening and milk. Blend well at lowest speed of mixer. Beat 1-1/2 minutes. Add egg and vanilla extract. Continue beating 1-1/2 minutes longer at low speed.

Pour batter into greased and floured 9" round pan. Bake for 30-35 minutes until cake is golden and springs back when lightly touched in center. This cake can also be baked in an 8" pan for 35 to 40 minutes. Allow cake to cool.

For icing, thoroughly combine Fluff, cream cheese and cherry juice, adjusting for taste. If it's too sweet, add more cream cheese. Ice cake and top with chopped fruit if desired.

Fluff mixture also makes a great fruit dip.

Irene Peterson says for somebody who hardly goes anywhere or does anything unique, she's managed to live a full life. She's been a WAC, teacher, truck driver, wife and mother, and now an author and editor. Her next release will be coming out around Halloween. Read more about Irene and her books at www.irenepeterson.com.

What's your recipe for a lasting, loving relationship?

Personally, I've been married to my Viking for thirty-seven years. The thing that I believe has kept us together is humor. We laugh a great deal. In fact, we laugh most of the time...well, not at funerals, though I had to stifle a laugh when his cremated cousin was brought into the chapel in a silver bucket. I thought my eyeballs were going to pop out from the pressure of holding in the guffaws. I never knew this cousin. It was a Mary Tyler Moore Chuckles the Clown reaction.

What's the best writing advice you ever received?

The best writing advice I ever received was that usual "write what you know" business. It doesn't necessarily mean only the boring things that happen around you. It means you can apply your accumulated life experience and knowledge to what you want to write. You don't have to be an astronaut to remember what claustrophobia feels like. You don't have to be dead to remember how powerful loss can be. Use what you have inside your head and heart and have a great story behind it all. Your characters will live much better for it.

Sue Viders: Lemon Meringue Pie

1/3 cup cornstarch
1-3/4 cups sugar
1-1/2 cups water
4 egg yolks, slightly beaten
1/4 cup lemon juice
2 tablespoons lightly salted butter
9" baked graham cracker pie shell
4 egg whites
1/2 teaspoon cream of tartar
1 cup sugar

Preheat oven to 400 F

To make the filling, combine cornstarch and 3/4 cup sugar in a small saucepan. Gradually add 1-1/2 cups of water, constantly stirring until smooth. Bring to a boil over medium heat. Keep stirring for about one minute or until mixture thickens. Quickly stir the egg yolks into the hot mixture, blending well. Bring to a boil for 1 minute, stirring continually. Remove from heat. Stir in lemon juice and butter, blending well. Pour immediately into the pie shell.

To make the meringue, in medium bowl with portable electric mixer at medium speed, beat egg whites with cream of tartar until soft peaks form when beater is raised. This takes several minutes or longer. Gradually beat in sugar, 2 tablespoons at a time. Continue to beat until stiff peaks form when beater is raised. Spread meringue over hot filling, carefully sealing to edge of crust.

Bake approximately 7-9 minutes or until the peaks of the meringue are golden. Cool for 1 hour before serving.

Sue Viders is the author of over twenty-five books, numerous articles and national columns. Her non-fiction includes *The Writer's Complete Guide to*

HEROES and HEROINES, Sixteen Master Archetypes, 10 Steps to Creating Memorable Characters, and *Deal a Story,* an interactive card game for writers that's based on the sixteen archetypes. She's also the author of the cozy mystery *Meg and the Mysterious Voices.*

She has been teaching writing for over thirty-five years both onsite, at various colleges and universities and national writing seminars, and online with writing organizations internationally. Her latest project is the *Whole Writing* Series, over two-dozen guides and workbooks for non-fiction and fiction aspiring writers. Sue no longer has a website or blog, but you can contact her at sueviders@comcast.net.

What's your recipe for a lasting, loving relationship?
I've been married for almost fifty-five years, have five adult children and six grandchildren. They all call and visit daily. I'm close to all of them. Sometimes I wish they all lived far away so I would have time to write, but they all know, or seem to believe, that I can fix anything and answer their life's pressing questions. Sigh.

I simply do the best I can in any situation and try to solve any problem that comes my way and in many cases their way. I like to think that given the problem, I can present all sides of the answer, then let them choose the best path to take.

After all, life happens, and it's how one copes with the difficult problems that arise that makes us who we are.

What's the best writing advice you ever received?
Get help.

I remember at one of my many art seminars I made reference to the fact that no one, if they want to be successful, lives on an island. We all need help of some kind. As I was speaking, an artist raised her hand and loudly spoke out, "Well, that's easy for you to say, but I live on an island." Grin.
No matter where you are in you writing journey, you will need some kind of

assistance. Perhaps it is a critique partner or a mentor who can give you advice.

I'm dyslexic. Can't spell very well (thank God for computers,) and I have no idea where to put the commas. But I do have ideas...lots and lots of ideas. I have learned to cope with my situation by writing with partners. The heroes and heroines book was co-written, as was the creating characters workbook.

My current project, *Whole Writer*, is being written with another talented writer who can "fix" my dyslexic mistakes. I also have a series of *Dottie Can Write* writing lectures coming out. And yes, I write those with another partner.

I needed help to become a successful writer. Without that help I doubt I could have written so many books or taught so many classes. And yes, I do write by myself, as I just did a Meg cozy, but then that also had help. Let's see...an editor, a proofreader, several beta groups, and finally a formatter.

So if you can't get off the island, get a few people to come for a short time to visit.

Liese Sherwood-Fabre: Basic Mexican Flan

A quick check into the history of flan indicates the Romans invented the custard dish. This population was the first to raise chickens for their eggs and developed a variety of custards using them. Most of these were not the sweet type that we know today. The Spaniards created a variation, adding caramelized sugar as a topping. The recipe involves mixing eggs, milk, and sugar and cooking in a baño María (bain-marie) where the mold holding the flan is set in a pan of water in the oven.

My mother-in-law gave this recipe to me, and I have found it to be a very easy, but delicious dessert. It does, however, require time to cook, then cool. As they would say in Mexico, ¡Provecho! (Enjoy!)

5 eggs, beaten
1 can sweetened condensed milk
whole milk, same amount as canned
1 tablespoon vanilla extract
granulated sugar
flan mold (can be individual ramekins or a larger one. I prefer a saucepan with an oven-proof handle)

Note: To lower the fat content, use fat-free sweetened condensed milk and skim milk.

Preheat oven to 350 degrees F.

Pour enough sugar into a saucepan to cover the bottom and heat on the stove, stirring constantly. When the sugar liquefies and turns brown, remove from heat (Be careful not to over-cook the caramelized sugar or it will tasted burned.) Pour the sugar into the bottom of the mold(s.)

While the sugar cools, place the eggs, the milks and vanilla extract into a blender and blend thoroughly. Pour the mixture into the mold(s) and set the mold(s) in a pan with water. Bake until set.
Allow to cool, then refrigerate. The mold can then be inverted onto a plate

and removed, letting the caramelized sugar syrup cover the top and sides.

Liese Sherwood-Fabre has won awards for her thrillers, romance, and literary short stories. *New York Times* bestselling author Steve Berry describes her writing as *"gimmick-free, old-fashioned storytelling."*

In the second grade, Liese knew she was destined to write when she received an A+ for her story about Dick, Jane, and Sally's ruined picnic. After obtaining her Ph.D. from Indiana University, she joined the federal government and had the opportunity to work and live internationally for more than fifteen years. She draws upon these experiences to endow her characters with deep conflicts and emotions. Read more about Liese and her books at www.liesesherwoodfabre.com.

What's your recipe for a lasting, loving relationship?

As I write this, I've been married thirty-three years. I wish I could pinpoint that *one* characteristic that has kept us together. If I could, I'd be running relationship seminars for oodles of money. What I have learned over the years, however, is that acceptance of differences goes a long way in keeping both partners committed.

My first major insight came when I read *Men are from Mars, Women are from Venus.* A lot of what I had experienced in my married life suddenly made sense. For years I had tried to find out what was upsetting my husband when he would grow silent and brooding. This book made me realize men tend to solve problems by thinking about them, and his reticence was related to wrestling with some issue he was facing in his life. Women prefer to talk about their problems with others—either to work them out or just to vent. Knowing and respecting these differences allows each partner to be themselves rather than trying to conform to another's ideas of acceptable behavior.

This leads to a corollary: Don't expect or try to change the other. Going into a relationship with the idea that you will be able to mold the other to your expectations will only lead to resentment and bitterness. No one likes to be pushed—even if they know it's for their own good. More likely than not, they will push back, and their behavior, attitude, appearance, or whatever it is you seek to change, will become more entrenched than ever.

My married life has weathered some crises neither of us anticipated, but we supported each other through them—in part because our different strengths were free to express themselves. They were just what we needed to be there for the other.

What's the best writing advice you ever received?
Readers read because they seek an emotional satisfaction from a book—be it rooting for a couple to overcome odds and be together, to stopping a villain from destroying the world, or someone coming to terms with who they are.

They care about the characters because they've formed an emotional bond on the very first page. In his book *Stein on Writing*, Sol Stein describes how one writer began a book with the character observing her nightly ritual of putting her son to bed before leaving to work as a police decoy. Throughout the rest of the book, Stein points out readers remember this woman as the mother of a small child and any danger she faces is heightened as a result.

While working on my novel *Saving Hope*, my creative writing professor noted in one lecture that if a story contains a child, she should be put in peril at some point. In one of those "light-bulb" moments, I put these two bits of advice together, and the whole basic structure of my plot unfolded. I rewrote the initial scene with a child's parents rushing her to the hospital after she contracts pneumonia. This child's critically needed medical care propels the mother into Russia's underworld. Her fight for her daughter's life culminates in the story's climax where the girl's life literally hangs in the balance.

This insight now directs me when I begin a story. What readers truly remember from a book are the characters and the story of their emotional journey. Get them to care about your characters at the beginning, and they will follow them anywhere.

Susan Santangelo: Ice Cream Bread

This two-ingredient bread is great any time of day. It can be prepared as a dessert topped with fresh fruit, whipped cream, chocolate, or other flavored sauces, or toasted and used as a side dish to a meal or for breakfast. The recipe is from Retirement Can Be Murder, *Book 1 of my Baby Boomer Mystery series.*

1 pint (2 cups) ice cream, softened. (Your choice of flavor but fruit flavors like peach or strawberry work very well.)
1-1/2 cups self-rising flour.

Preheat oven to 350 degrees F.

Stir ingredients together just enough so that flour is thoroughly moistened. Spoon batter into 4" x 8" loaf pan. Bake for 40-45 minutes or until a wooden toothpick inserted in the center of the bread comes out clean. Remove bread from pan and cool on a wire rack.

Susan Santangelo, an early member of the Baby Boomer generation, is the author of the humorous Baby Boomer mystery series (*Retirement Can Be Murder, Moving Can Be Murder, Marriage Can Be Murder, Class Reunions Can Be Murder*, and *Funerals Can Be Murder.*) She is currently working on the sixth book in the series, *Second Honeymoons Can Be Murder.*

Susan divides her time between Cape Cod, MA and the Connecticut shoreline. She's a member of Sisters in Crime and the Cape Cod Writers Center and shares her life with her husband Joe and one very spoiled English cocker spaniel, Boomer, who also serves as the model for the books' covers.

A portion of the sales from the Baby Boomer Mysteries is donated to the Breast Cancer Survival Center, a non-profit organization based in Connecticut, which Susan founded in 1999 after she was diagnosed with cancer. Read more about Susan at www.babyboomermysteries.com.

What's your recipe for a lasting, loving relationship?

The protagonists in my series, Carol and Jim Andrews, have been married for over thirty-five years. In *Moving Can Be Murder*, Carol comes up with an ingenious idea to improve their relationship—a "Honey *Don't* List," a variation on the traditional "Honey Do List." Here's how it works: Each partner in a relationship prepares a list of the other's habits/faults that are really irritating. (Carol points out that her list is much shorter than Jim's.) The list is separated into individual pieces and put into two containers—His and Hers. At the beginning of the week, each partner chooses one habit from the other's container (eyes shut and no peeking!) and has to refrain from that behavior for the entire week. Whichever partner behaves the best gets to pick a reward at the end of the week. Carol likes going out to an expensive restaurant. Jim likes...well, you can figure that part out for yourself!

What's the best writing advice you ever received?

Know who your ideal audience/customer is, and write for that audience.

Sheila Seabrook: Banana Nut Bread

1 cup white flour
1 cup whole wheat flour
1/2 cup granulated sugar
3 teaspoons baking powder
1/2 teaspoon baking soda
3/4 cup skim milk
1/4 cup vegetable oil
1 egg
1-2 ripe bananas (when doubling recipe, use 3 bananas)
handful of walnut halves

Preheat oven to 350 degrees F.

In a large bowl, sift together flours, sugar, baking powder, and baking soda.

Place the skim milk, vegetable oil, egg, and bananas into a blender. Blend until smooth, then add the walnuts and blend using the chop or grind function.

Pour liquid ingredients over the dry ingredients and mix well. Turn into greased 9" x 5" x 3" loaf pan. Bake 65-70 minutes or until toothpick inserted into center comes out clean.

Sheila Seabrook writes contemporary romance and humorous romantic women's fiction from her home on the Canadian prairies. Her emotional stories are filled with smart, sassy heroines, hot heroes who make them laugh, and a wild assortment of family members guaranteed to try to steal the show. Needless to say, Sheila has decreed that every hero and heroine's journey must end on a happily-ever-after note. Her titles include *Always Remember*, *Terms of Surrender*, and *Wedding Fever*.

When Sheila's not writing, emailing her readers, or exchanging texts with her siblings, she can be found staring out the office window watching the wildlife wander through her yard. Read more about Sheila and her books at www.sheilaseabrook.com.

What's your recipe for a lasting, loving relationship?
Always treat everyone with understanding, compassion, and kindness.

What's the best writing advice you ever received?
Write a great book. Rinse and repeat.

Lisa Verge Higgins: Rum Pecan Pie

Full confession: I love to eat, but I'm a lazy cook. Life is too short to spend slaving in the kitchen when there are books to read and write. I love this recipe not only because the pie is delicious—especially served slightly warm with whipped cream—but because the recipe is of the mix-it-all-up-and-bake-it kind. Plus, once the rum is on the table, can cocktail hour be far behind?

1 pie crust (store-bought is fine)
3 large eggs
5-1/3 tablespoons salted butter, melted
1 cup white sugar
1 cup dark or light corn syrup
1 cup pecan halves
2 tablespoons rum

Preheat oven to 350 degrees F.

Grease a pie plate, then line it with the pie crust.

Mix the rest of the ingredients well and pour into the crust. Crimp the edges.

Place the pie on a cookie sheet and bake for about 45 minutes. When done, the center will be jiggly, but not liquid. Sip on a fresh Rum Runner while you're waiting for the pie to cool enough for serving.

Lisa Verge Higgins is the critically acclaimed RITA-nominated author of sixteen novels that have been published worldwide and translated into as many languages—quite a switch for this former chemist. She started her career as Lisa Ann Verge, writing emotionally intense romance about hot men and dangerous women, and now writes life-affirming women's fiction as Lisa Verge Higgins. A finalist for *Romantic Times'* book awards five times over, Lisa has won the Golden Leaf and the Bean Pot and has twice cracked Barnes & Noble's General Fiction Forum's Top Twenty Books of the Year.
Lisa currently lives in New Jersey with her husband and their three daughters,

who never fail to make life interesting. Read more about Lisa and her books at www.lisavergehiggins.com.

What's your recipe for a lasting friendship?
I called it "the Great Diaspora," that moment in my twenties when my tight-knit group of college friends started leaving The Big City for new jobs, new adventures, new romantic relationships, or a house in the suburbs for the new baby. Soon marriage, mortgages and maternity focused our time and attention elsewhere, and it seemed years passed between phone calls. It took us a while to get back on track, mostly because of this recipe:

One part *keeping in touch, even briefly.* Facebook and Twitter are a godsend, but birthday cards have that personal touch. Text when you see a new book out by your friend's favorite author. Instagram a photo of their favorite drink as you enjoy it with them in mind. Will you have an extended layover in a nearby airport? Invite them out for coffee. Small efforts like this keep the friendship alive during those stretches when time is at a premium.

One part *empathy.* Life is long and full of ups and downs. Those friends who are present when times are bad, as well as when times are good, are the true keepers. Make an extra effort to show sympathy and understanding as well as joy.

One part *marking milestones.* Make the extra effort to attend those weddings and be present for the funerals. Make time to get together to celebrate landmark birthdays. Repeat often, or else your friendship will take on an archival quality.

What's the best writing advice you ever received?
Risk, risk, risk. I remember very little from my college graduation except this refrain from the great journalist Jim Lehrer, who spoke at commencement. He was exhorting all of us freshly minted graduates to go forth and take chances in our careers and in our lives—to forgo the fear of failure and walk that road less traveled. When, a few years later, I had to choose between two different careers, I chose the riskier path—the career of a novelist. I still hear his

words—*risk risk risk*—every time I sit down in front of my computer. Life isn't meant to be played safe, and neither is writing. It's only when we take creative risks that we grow.

Elaine Charton: Low-Cal Better than Sex Cake

Chocolate cake mix and pudding can be substituted for yellow cake and vanilla pudding.

1 box yellow cake mix
applesauce in amount needed to substitute for oil
2 boxes sugar-free French vanilla pudding
milk in quantity specified on pudding packages
20 ounce can crushed pineapple in its own juice
16 ounces Cool Whip
1 cup Splenda
1cup toasted, sweetened coconut flakes (optional)

Preheat oven to 350 degrees F.

Prepare cake mix according to directions, substituting applesauce for oil. Pour in a 9" x 13" greased pan and bake as directed on package.

Remove from oven and let cool. Poke holes in cake with fork.

Make pudding according to directions and allow to sit.

Pour pineapple and juice in saucepan. Add Splenda and cook over low heat until Splenda is dissolved.

Pour pineapple over cake. Spread pudding over top of cake. Cover with foil and refrigerate at least 2 hours (can leave over night.)

Frost with Cool Whip. Sprinkle with optional coconut flakes.

Elaine Charton, who also writes as Elaine Joyce, has had a book in her hand for as long as she can remember. She should have realized it would be only a matter of time before she began writing her own stories. Born in Boston, Massachusetts, she met her husband, also a writer, on a blind date. They fell in love over a shared interest in books, Chinese food, and baseball. Theirs is a mixed marriage—she's a Red Sox Fan; he's a Mets fan. They live in the Arizona desert with two very spoiled cats.

Elaine's books include *Mac's Man, The Pink Lady, The Man in the Mirror, Dead Men Do Tell Tales*, and *Murder on Dark Fort Isle*. Read more about Elaine and her books at www.echartonwrites.wix.com/chartons-corner.

What's your recipe for a lasting, loving relationship?

My grandmother told me something once that I have never forgotten. My grandparents were married over fifty years and she said, "There were times I was wishing he was in hell, and times he was wishing I was in hell. It still was the best years of my life."

There will be times you may not like your spouse, but you always love him. We recently celebrated our thirtieth anniversary and believe any long-lasting relationship has to be worth the effort taken to make it last. My husband is my best friend, and I know he has my back and I have his.

What's the best writing advice you ever received?

There were actually two pieces of advice: Give yourself permission to write garbage. Under that garbage may be pure gold. The ultimate thing is to get your words on paper. Editing that first draft will get rid of the garbage and leave the gold. And don't be afraid to step out of your comfort zone. You may be pleasantly surprised where it will lead you.

Sharleen Scott: Berries and Cream Pie

A simple recipe using your favorite combination of berries

4 cups berries (fresh or thawed)
9" pre-made pie crust
2/3 cup sugar
4 tablespoons flour
1/4 teaspoon salt
1/2 teaspoon cinnamon
1 cup cream or half-and-half

Preheat oven to 400 degrees F.

Place berries in pie crust. Mix remaining ingredients. Pour mixture over berries.

Bake for 35–45 minutes. Center should be set. (Blueberries may require a longer baking time.)

Sharleen Scott lives in the foothills of the Cascade Mountains in Washington State where she writes contemporary romance/mystery/suspense and women's fiction. Her debut novel, *Caught in Cross Seas*, features a country music hero, a bakery owner/homeless advocate heroine in plaid Converse All Stars, a colorful cast of extras, and possibly a serial killer. Her second novel, *Caught in the Spin*, features a retired bull rider/single dad hero, a single mom heroine on the run, a psychotic ex-husband, and a ghost. It will be released in October 2014. Read more about Sharleen and her books at www.sharleenscott.com.

What's your recipe for a lasting, loving relationship?
I come from a long line of golden-wedding-anniversary-celebrating ancestors, and I have the genealogy records to prove it. My husband and I will celebrate our thirtieth anniversary the same month my parents will celebrate sixty years of wedded bliss. My grandparents had sixty-eight wonderful years together.

Does this give me license to offer relationship advice? I've been watching matrimonial paradise at close range for a long time and have observed a thing or two:

1. Don't be in a hurry. Wait for the right person to come along. You'll know who that person is when it happens.

2. Make sure you can talk to each other. Picture the two of you in fifty to sixty years. Conversation is looking a little more important, isn't it?

3. Share your lives. Share your interests. It isn't necessary to have all the same interests, but it helps the relationship when each takes an interest in the other's activities.

4. Respect each other. Understand that you won't always be right and neither will he.

5. Hold hands when you walk into the grocery store. It's the little things that count.

6. Watch the sunset together every chance you get.

7. Be thankful you found each other and enjoy!

What's the best writing advice you ever received?

Write from the heart. New writers are sometimes tempted to follow trends, thinking that's a surefire way to success, but it isn't necessarily so. Let's say the bestsellers' lists are full of vampire-troll romances. You don't necessarily like vampire-trolls, maybe even find the idea creepy, but everyone is selling a bazillion vampire-troll romances, indicating it must be the thing to write. You spend many months, maybe years, from first draft to finished product delving into the complex world of vampire-trolls.

By the time you emerge from your writing haze, the vampire-troll craze has become cliché, and there's a new game in town: Navy SEAL-faerie, time-travel romances set in pre-WWII Bolivia. Do you sit down to write one? No. You follow your heart and write the story that has been yelling from the back of your brain, "Write me. I beg you. Write me." You set aside all those ideas of the easy road to success through bestseller emulation and realize you have to write *your* book. You have to tap into your emotions, write your truth, and allow yourself to be taken for a thrill ride. It will probably take longer, but in the end, you'll have written *your* book. Follow your heart, because only a book written from the heart will have heart. And isn't that what romances are all about?

Kathy Bennett: Homicide For the Hips Easy English Toffee

1 cup nuts of your choice, chopped
1 stick butter plus a little for greasing dish
3/4 cup brown sugar
1 cup chocolate chips

Lightly butter a 5" x 7" baking dish and sprinkle it with chopped nuts.

In a small saucepan, boil butter and brown sugar for 7 minutes, stirring constantly. Pour the butter/brown sugar mixture over the nuts and sprinkle with chocolate chips. Cover the baking dish until the chocolate chips melt (approximately 5 minutes.) Remove the cover and spread the chocolate chips over the brown sugar mixture. Let pan sit until cool.

Kathy Bennett served twenty-nine years with the Los Angeles Police Department, eight as a civilian employee and twenty-one years as a sworn police officer. Most of her career was spent in a patrol car, but other assignments included: Firearms Instructor at the LAPD Academy, crime analyst, Field Training Officer, Senior Lead Officer, and working undercover in various assignments. Kathy was named Officer of the Year in 1997.

Kathy's debut novel, *A Dozen Deadly Roses*, and her second book, *A Deadly Blessing*, became bestselling e-books at Amazon and Barnes & Noble. *A Deadly Blessing* was selected by Barnes & Noble as a Best Book of 2012. Her third book, *A Deadly Justice*, became a bestselling police procedural novel. Her latest book in the Detective Maddie Divine series is *A Deadly Denial*.
Law enforcement personnel laud Kathy's authentic stories of crime and suspense for "getting it right." Read more about Kathy and her books at www.KathyBennett.com.

What's your recipe for a lasting, loving relationship?
I've done marriage wrong before, so now that I've finally got it right, I think

235

these are the key ingredients for a happy, loving relationship: I think you need a big bowl of trust, blend in respect for each other, and sift in laughter, making sure you're able to laugh at yourself, too.

What's the best writing advice you ever received?

If you've got a sentence or a paragraph that isn't working and you've tried and tried to fix, it and it still isn't working, you probably don't need that sentence or paragraph at all.

Jody Payne: Chocolate Zucchini Brownies

My DH doesn't eat vegetables. Never. So our sweetest daughter-in-love found this recipe. He has no idea it might actually be good for him. Bless his heart.

1/2 cup coconut oil
1/2 cup unsalted butter
1-3/4 cups sugar
1/2 cup buttermilk
2-1/2 cups flour
2 eggs
1 teaspoon vanilla extract (Mexican, if you can get it)
4 tablespoons cocoa
1 teaspoon baking soda
1/2 teaspoon cinnamon
1/2 teaspoon salt
1/2 cup chopped nuts
1/2 cup chocolate chips
2 cups grated zucchini (don't peel)

Preheat oven to 350 degrees F.

In large mixing bowl, combine oil, butter, sugar, eggs, and vanilla extract. Add milk and dry ingredients. Mix until smooth. Stir in grated zucchini. Pour into greased and floured 9" x 13" pan. Sprinkle top with nuts and chocolate chips. Bake for 35-40 minutes.

Jody Payne is from a long line of storytellers. Growing up, she remembers jasmine-scented nights on the porch listening to tales about past family. Some of it was probably even true. They taught her this: Never let the truth get in the way of a good story.

Could it possibly be true her great-grandfather stole a neighbor's pig and dressed him up like a little boy to fool the sheriff? That was one of the more believable tales. The one about vampires living in the hayloft she absolutely never believed. She just didn't care to go up there, anyway. Is it any wonder she writes stories about the south?

Jody's books include *Forget the Rules* and *Flashpoint*. She's also the author of the short *Rendezvous*. Read more about Jody and her books at www.jodypayne.net.

What's your recipe for a lasting, loving relationship?

One thing I've come to accept over the years is communication is highly overrated. Even if you talk until your throat feels like you've swallowed a scorpion, he won't get it. Go buy some really pricey ice cream, one of those designer brands, and rent a chick flick. This advice only applies if you can't afford a long weekend at a spa. I've heard that works wonders, but that's only hearsay. I can't even afford the good ice cream.

And that bit about never go to bed angry? Girlfriend, it won't make a bit of difference. He won't even know you're still angry, and if you tell him, he'll be puzzled as to why.

I guess what I want to tell you about marriage is this: He's a man. He doesn't think like a woman, and he never will. But come on, do you really want him to? Cherish the difference.

I should have warned you, I don't know a thing about marriage. I have nothing to compare it with since I've been married so long. I don't remember much about being single. And I'm happy with that. For this and other ridiculously bad advice, visit my website.

What's the best writing advice you ever received?

The best advice I've ever received about writing is kind of odd, and I still can't always follow it. Okay, almost never. Don't assume that someone else knows best. Every time I enter a contest, I slavishly follow the judge's advice and change everything. The poor manuscript ends up as a composite of many voices, meaning none. So unless everyone is saying the same thing about your manuscript, go with your gut.

Reggi Allder: Holiday Almond Bundt Cake Recipe

This cake can be used for any holiday, even the Super Bowl. Just change the icing and decorations to match the occasion i.e. pastel sugar circles for a birthday, a flag for Fourth of July, or green and/or red sugar sprinkles for Christmas. If you're creative, use marzipan and food coloring to create angels or a Santa Claus. For sporting events ice the cake in the color of your favorite team. The cake travels well, so it's easy to take to an event.

2-1/2 cups pastry flour

1/2 cup finely ground natural almonds (not roasted or salted)

2 cups sugar

1-1/4 tablespoons baking powder

1-1/2 cups half and half or cream, plus additional 2 or more tablespoons

2/3 cup butter, softened

1-3/4 teaspoons pure almond extract

3 egg whites

1 cup confectioner's sugar

2 or more tablespoons of half and half or cream

Preheat oven at 350 degrees F.

Note: Almonds should be ground to the consistency flour.

Mix together flour, ground almonds, sugar, and baking powder. Add 1-1/2 cups cream, butter, and 1-1/2 teaspoons almond extract. Beat until completely mixed and smooth.

In a separate bowl beat egg whites. Add to batter and beat until fully combined, about two minutes.

Pour batter into greased bundt pan. Bake for 30-35 minutes or until a toothpick or a knife blade inserted into cake comes out clean.
Remove from oven and allow to cool 10-15 minutes. Remove from pan. Allow cake to cool completely before icing, at least 2-1/2 hours.

To make icing, mix together confectioner's sugar and 1/4 teaspoon almond extract, then slowly stir in 2 tablespoons cream. Add just enough cream to make the icing thin enough to easily drizzle down the cake. While the icing is still wet, if desired, add decorations around the top of the cake.

Reggi Allder, author of romantic suspense and contemporary romance novels, likes nothing better than writing tales of love lost, then found. That and telling stories of heroes and heroines who discover love but wonder if they'll live long enough to enjoy it. She studied screen writing and creative writing at UCLA and was a chapter president of Romance Writers of America. She's worked as a newsletter editor, an advertising manager, and as part of the support staff in a large city hospital. Her various career moves and experiences now help her craft her books.

Food also plays a key role in two of her novels. *Her Country Heart*, her new contemporary romance, will be available soon and features her grandmother's favorite apple pie recipe. Reggi's other books include *Money Power and Poison* and *Shattered Rules*. Read more about Reggi at www.reggiallder.com.

What's your recipe for a lasting, loving relationship?
Be good to each other; you are on the same team. Say, "I love you." Have a regular date night without smart phones. It doesn't have to be expensive. Go for a walk and hold hands. Keep a sense of humor. Life is busy, complicated, and stressful. Humor can take the sting out of many difficult situations. Stay faithful even when confronted with temptation. Always remember why you fell in love. Keep the heat in the relationship; take time to reconnect.

What's the best writing advice you ever received?
Don't worry. Just write it down. You can always edit.

Ashlyn Chase: High-Protein, Low-Carb Chocolate Cupcakes

I just lost forty-four pounds, and I did that on a low-carb, high-protein diet. I found something called CarbThin ZeroCarb Soy Protein Bake Mix online. It calls for some unusual ingredients, but I'm lazy and finding the baking mix was enough effort for me. So, everything else can be bought at the grocery store.

Eat one of these cupcakes while reading The Cupcake Coven.

3 scoops chocolate CarbThin soy protein bake mix
2 teaspoons baking powder
1/4 cup sugar substitute (I used Stevia)
4 teaspoons reconstituted powdered egg whites or 4 egg whites
1/4 cup warm water
2 tablespoons sugar-free chocolate syrup
2 eggs
1/3 cup butter substitute (like I Can't Believe It's Not Butter)

Preheat oven to 350 degrees F.

Combine the bake mix, baking powder, and sugar substitute.

Whip the egg whites and set aside.

Combine the water, chocolate syrup, eggs, and butter substitute. Mix with dry ingredients. Fold in whipped egg whites.

Use PAM or non-stick spray on cupcake tins or use parchment liners. Bake for 18 minutes.

Ashlyn Chase describes herself as an Almond Joy bar—a little nutty, a little flaky, but basically sweet, and wanting only to give her readers a satisfying experience.

She holds a degree in behavioral sciences, worked as a psychiatric RN for several years, and spent a few more years working for the American Red Cross. She credits her sense of humor to her former careers since comedy helped preserve whatever was left of her sanity. She is a multi-published, award-winning author of humorous erotic and paranormal romances.

Ashlyn lives in beautiful New Hampshire with her true-life hero husband of twenty years, who looks like Hugh Jackman with a salt and pepper dye job. The couple is owned by a spoiled-brat cat. Read more about Ashlyn and her books at www.ashlynchase.com.

What's your recipe for a lasting, loving relationship?
Humor and respect. It's great to joke around and tease each other, but never let it hurt your loved one.

What's the best writing advice you ever received?
Finish the book, polish, submit, and repeat. If the first one doesn't sell, maybe the second will, or the third. Just keep writing and improving with each effort.

Beverley Bateman: Sweet Story Cake

2-1/2 cups white flour

1-1/2 cups sugar

3-1/2 teaspoons baking powder

1 teaspoon salt

1/2 cup cooking oil

20 cherries (canned or fresh)

3/4 cup whole milk

1/4 cup cherry juice

1 teaspoon vanilla extract

1-1/2 teaspoons almond extract

4 egg whites

2/3 cup walnuts (optional)

2 cups confectioner's sugar

1/2 cup shortening

2 tablespoons water

1-1/2 teaspoons red food coloring

Preheat oven to 375 degrees F.

Mix flour, sugar, salt and baking powder. Add cooking oil, milk, cherry juice, and vanilla and almond extracts. Beat two minutes. Add egg whites and beat two more minutes.

Fold in cherries and nuts.

Pour batter into grease 9" x 13" pan. Bake 20-25 minutes. Cool.

To make optional frosting, combine in a mixer confectioner's sugar, shortening, water, and food coloring. Blend until all ingredients are thoroughly mixed.

Beverley Bateman is a Canadian who lives with her husband and two Shiba

Ina dogs in the Okanagan Valley in British Columbia, an area filled with beautiful mountains, lakes, and beaches. The area also produces world class wines, which she feels obliged to sip on a regular basis while writing her romantic suspense and medical thrillers. Her latest books include the Hawkins' Family series (*Hunted* and *Missing*) and her Assistant PI Holly Devine series (*A Cruise to Remember* and *A Murder to Forget*.) Read more about Beverley and her books at www.beverleybateman.com.

What's your recipe for a lasting, loving relationship?
I thought about writing about my wonderful husband, but then I thought of some wonderful friendships I've had with girlfriends for longer than I've been with my husband. While you choose a husband, or significant other, you have to work at the relationship to make it work. At least that's my experience.

My female friends are wonderful women who I've been friends with for many years. It's not an effort; we're always there for each other—no matter what. What makes it work? Here's my recipe for a lasting, loving friendship:

Start with 2 cups of genuinely liking the person. Then add the following:
2 large cups of acceptance
2 cups of non-judgmental attitude
2 cups of laughter (frequent, loud, and to the point of tears recommended)
2 cups of big hugs, done often
2 cups of being there whenever you need a shoulder to cry on, a word of encouragement or a "way to go"
2 cups of no apologies needs
2 cups of honesty

Mix all together and you've got a lifelong, warm, and giving friendship—BFFs forever.

What's the best writing advice you ever received?
For me it's the Ten Minute Rule. A year or two ago I was blocked. I wasn't writing. Life kept interfering, and I couldn't find time to sit down to write. I took a class geared to motivating yourself to write. We were assigned partners.

The class was very good, but I still wasn't writing, except for class assignments. My partner and I talked about it, and I explained I never had time. She asked if I had ten minutes I could find somewhere. I said I guessed so. She said I didn't need to write one, two, three hours a day. Ten minutes would be fine. And I needed to be accountable for the ten minutes.

So I wrote ten minutes before I went to bed, then sent her an email to let her know I had done it. Pretty soon those ten minutes grew to twenty, then thirty, until I was writing whenever I got the chance. Every time I think I don't have time to write, I remember the Ten Minute Rule. It works every time.

Susan Lohrer: Grandma's Homemade Brownies

For a lower-calorie version, you can substitute applesauce for half the cooking oil, but I suggest simply cutting the brownies into tiny portions.

1-1/2 cups all-purpose flour
1 teaspoon salt
2 cups sugar
1/2 cup cocoa
2 teaspoons vanilla extract
1 cup vegetable oil
4 eggs
1/4 cup cool water
1/2 cup (or more) chopped nuts, raisins, or dried cherries

Preheat oven to 350 degrees F.

Place all ingredients in bowl in order given and beat on low speed until just mixed. Pour batter into prepared 9" x13" pan.
Bake for 30 minutes or until toothpick inserted in brownies comes out clean.

Susan Lohrer is a contemporary romance author who grew up in more towns in western Canada than she has fingers to count them on. She currently lives in southern British Columbia with her husband of more than two decades, their two teenagers who are still at home, three dogs, and far more aquariums than a reasonable household should contain. She believes life—and books— are always better with a healthy dose of humor. Susan is the author of *Rocky Road* and *Over the Edge*. Read more about Susan and her books at www.susanlohrer.com.

What's your recipe for a lasting, loving relationship?
1. Respect
2. Commitment
3. Trust
4. Friendship

5. A sense of adventure

6. A sense of humor

7. Physical attraction

Add all of the above in the order given and stir constantly for as long as you both shall live.

You may be wondering why *love* isn't on that list and *physical attraction* isn't first. For a romantic relationship to endure, you have to start with respect. If your partner is the hottest McHotterson ever, but you feel irritated by his/her mere presence, the relationship isn't going to go anywhere. Respect is the ingredient that binds the relationship together. If you have a profound respect for one another, enjoy spending time together, and fully trust your emotional wellbeing in your partner's hands, you'll find a deep, abiding love that keeps growing with the years.

Physical attraction is an important ingredient in a relationship (of course it is—and it's often the thing that brings two people together initially,) but a relationship isn't just physical—and actually, the mind is the most powerful sex organ. And as for love: love isn't a mere ingredient in a relationship. Love is the product of a lifetime of nurturing that relationship; you might even say it's the dessert. As for the sense of humor...well, you can equate that to the nuts in the brownies—it's not strictly essential, but it definitely makes things a lot more fun.

What's the best writing advice you ever received?

As a wife, mother, grandmother, and businessperson, I often struggle with making time to write, and so the piece of writing advice that strikes home for me speaks to that struggle: *"If you feel you need permission to do all the reading and writing your little heart desires, however, consider it hereby granted by yours truly."* (Stephen King, *On Writing*)

Donis Casey: Chocolate Gravy

When I was a girl, my sister and I would occasionally spend the night at my cousin's house in Haskell, Oklahoma. In the morning, my aunt would treat us to a breakfast of biscuits and chocolate gravy. Now, I was fond of my cousin, but I loved that chocolate gravy. I don't know where my aunt came up with the recipe. I've never known of anyone else who made it. There is a recipe for a particularly intense chocolate pudding and pie filling that has been passed down in my mother's family, and I suspect that the gravy may be a variation thereon. I seldom make the gravy myself these days, since it is hardly a health food. It is, however, delicious, and tastes to me of summer days and youth.

1 to 1-1/2 generous tablespoons butter (If using unsalted butter, add a pinch of salt to recipe)
2 rounded tablespoons all-purpose flour
2 cups milk (whole milk is best, but 2% is fine)
1/2 cup sugar (or more to taste)
1/2 cup unsweetened Baker's cocoa
1 teaspoon vanilla extract and/or cinnamon

Melt butter in a saucepan. To make a roux, add the flour to the melted butter and whisk together until smooth and bubbly. Slowly pour the milk into the pan, whisking continually. Bring to low boil over medium heat. Simmer and stir until mixture begins to cling to the back of a spoon.

Add the sugar all at once, then the cocoa. Reduce heat to medium-low. Continue to whisk until smooth, well blended and thickened to the consistency of cream gravy. Stir in optional vanilla extract and/or cinnamon if desired. Remove from heat and let stand for five minutes before serving.

I use butter for the fat, but my aunt actually used bacon drippings. This sounds unlikely, but it's a surprisingly sumptuous combination.

In my family, the gravy is traditionally ladled over fat, fluffy, homemade biscuits for breakfast, but it's also good hot or cold over angel cake or as a fruit dip. Leftover gravy can be refrigerated for several days. It will thicken to the consistency of a thin pudding.

Donis Casey is the author of the Alafair Tucker Mysteries, set in Oklahoma in the booming 1910s and featuring the sleuthing mother of ten children. To date, seven novels in the series have been published, including *The Old Buzzard Had It Coming*, *Hornswoggled*, *The Drop Edge of Yonder*, *The Sky Took Him*, *Crying Blood*, *The Wrong Hill to Die On*, and *Hell With the Lid Blown Off*.

Donis has twice won the Arizona Book Award and has been a finalist for the Willa Award and a five-time finalist for the Oklahoma Book Award. Her first novel, *The Old Buzzard Had It Coming*, was named an Oklahoma Centennial Book. Read more about Donis and her books at www.doniscasey.com.

What's Your Recipe for a Lasting, Loving Relationship?

I have been married for a long, long time. We have been through some very bad stuff together, had some epic rows, a lot of laughs and fun, several triumphs, and our share of sweaty nights. In the end it has worked out very well and is one of the great sources of joy in my life. But when people ask what our secret is, I'm hesitant to offer advice because what do I know?

I've seen many a successful relationship that I couldn't stand to live in, myself. But everyone has different needs and if it works, it works. In the end, all I can say is that over the years I've learned what works for us:

You can't make your partner responsible for your happiness. It isn't fair. It isn't even possible. If you try, you're doomed to be unhappy.

A relationship is like the weather in Oklahoma. You'll have long, gorgeous summer days followed by terrible storms. A stretch of dreary clouds and drizzle after which the sun breaks through and everything is clean and beautiful and bursts into bloom. You can't control the weather or a relationship, either. But you can count on the fact that it will change.

Eventually, you'll hurt each other and act like idiots. If you're the hurter, get over yourself and ask for forgiveness. If you're the hurtee, forgive and let it go. If you hang on to resentment, the person you'll punish most is yourself.

My mother always said that if you want to be loved, you have to be loving, and you ought to try to be lovable.

What's the Best Writing Advice You Every Received?
Very early on in my life, one of my college writing instructors said, "You can't edit a blank page."

The most important thing you can do as a writer is get the words down on the page, because as the old saw goes, writing is rewriting. There may be an authorly Mozart out there somewhere whose every word of his first draft is a perfect gem, but I've never met him. Probably because he doesn't exist. A Very Famous Author once told me that her first draft is always crap (her word.) I suspect that William Shakespeare's first draft was always crap.

Allow me to relate one of my favorite metaphorical illustrations, which anyone who has known me for five minutes has heard me tell—because it's so perfect:

I am sure you have heard the story of the man who asked Michelangelo how he managed to create such a magnificent work of art as his statue of David out of something as featureless as a block of marble. Michelangelo replied, "Easy. I just chipped away everything that didn't look like David."

Writing is exactly the same. You absolutely can create a literary David, but first you have to have that block of marble to work with. Get it down, even if it's crap. Then you can go back and chip away everything that doesn't look like David.

Barbara Fass Leavy: Chocolate-Chambord Bundt Cake

This cake can be made with an optional 4" sharp file baked into the center. Bring the cake to an unfairly convicted prisoner you hope will break out of jail and search for the real culprit.

1 box dark chocolate cake mix (without pudding in mix)
1/2 cup canola oil
1 cup Chambord
4 eggs at room temperature
1 cup sour cream
1 box instant chocolate pudding (not pudding that must be cooked)
8 tablespoons butter
3/4 cup sugar
whipped cream
fresh strawberries

Preheat oven to 350 degrees F.

Pour cake mix into large bowl. Beat in oil, 1/2 cup Chambord, eggs, sour cream, and chocolate pudding mix in that order. Pour into greased bundt or ring cake pan. Bake for 1 hour and test with toothpick to see if it comes out clean. Place on rack to cool but don't remove from pan.

While cake is baking, mix together 1/2 cup Chambord, butter, and sugar in saucepan. Boil for 2-3 minutes. Allow to cool. Skim off butter solids that might have risen to top

Prick cake with fork in many places. With a spoon, dribble syrup over cake, allowing it to seep through. Allow cake to sit for 30 minutes. Invert onto cake platter. Fill hole in center of cake with whipped cream and garnish with raspberries

Barbara Fass Leavy regularly writes features on mysteries. Her book-length study, *The Fiction of Ruth Rendell: Ancient Tragedy and the Modern Family*, includes an analysis of Rendell's treatment of food, feasts, meals, and eating disorders. There are no specific recipes involved but one of her characters and perhaps murderer gorges on sweets (*Heartstones*) and might try to consume this Chocolate-Chambord cake in a single sitting. Read more about Barbara and her writing at www.barbaraleavy.com.

What's your recipe for a lasting, loving relationship?
Treat your significant other with the same courtesy you would have when you first met. If something helpful or loving is done for you, say "thank you" or "I really appreciate that" or "how nice!" Do not take the loving act for granted.

What's the best writing advice you ever received?
Of course, I write non-fiction but capturing my readers is still absolutely necessary if they are to continue reading what I write. I was advised to let my reader know from the very beginning where my discussion and analysis were going. Do not save your major ideas for last, I was told, as if the solution to a mystery. Surprise, surprise! Look where we are.

Stacy Juba: Tiramisu

My great-aunt, who was born in Italy, gave me this recipe. Traditionally, tiramisu is made from ladyfingers dipped in coffee, and layered with a whipped mixture of eggs, sugar and mascarpone cheese flavored with cocoa. This version has much sweeter layers.

shortening
1 box chocolate cake mix
2 boxes chocolate instant pudding
7 Heath Bars or package of crushed Heath Bar
16 ounces Cool Whip (2 small containers)

Preheat oven according to directions on cake mix box.

Grease bottoms and sides of cake pan with shortening. Prepare cake mix following recipe on box and bake. Allow cake to cool.

Make chocolate pudding following the directions on box. Keep pudding at room temperature.

Place Heath Bars in zip lock bag and crush with rolling pin, unless using a package of already crushed Heath Bars. Crumble up cake into chunks and set aside. In a large glass trifle dish, layer half of the crumbled cake, half the pudding, 8 ounces Cool Whip, and half of the Heath bar candy. Repeat layers. Refrigerate.

Stacy Juba loves to write stories about characters at a crossroads: individuals who are finding themselves and getting on the right life path after overcoming obstacles. She's written about reality TV contestants targeted by a killer, an obit writer investigating a cold case, teen psychics who control minds, twin high school hockey stars battling on the ice, and teddy bears learning to raise the U.S. flag.

Stacy has made numerous bestseller lists, including GalleyCat's Barnes &

Noble Bestsellers and GalleyCat's Mystery and Thriller Bestsellers. She's had a book ranked #5 in the Nook Store and #30 on the Amazon Kindle Paid List. Her titles include the adult mystery novels *Twenty-Five Years Ago Today* and *Sink or Swim*, the chick lit novel *Fooling Around With Cinderella*, the YA novels *Face-Off* and *Dark Before Dawn*, and the children's book *The Flag Keeper*.

Stacy also offers a beta reading/editing service for writers. Read more about Stacy and her books at www.stacyjuba.com.

What's your recipe for a lasting, loving relationship?
Understanding
Fun
Laughter
Romance

Understanding: One of the most important things is to understand the other person's viewpoint, even if you don't agree with it. Respect that you both come from different backgrounds and have different personalities and see the world through your own perspectives. Listen to your partner's side and calmly explain your own side. See if there is some way you can compromise.

Fun: No matter how busy the two of you are, always make time for each other. Go out to dinner and a movie, or if it's hard to find babysitters, rent a video, make popcorn, and have a stay-in movie night.

Laughter: If something funny happened during your day, make a mental note to tell your partner. Watch sitcoms together, tease each other, and share a chuckle over a funny video on You Tube. Find ways to inject a dose of humor into your day.

Romance: Kiss each other at least once every day. Don't skimp on this ingredient.

What's the best writing advice you ever received?

The best writing advice I ever received was to work hard on building a compelling setting for my new Storybook Valley chick lit contemporary romance series. The series is set at a theme park, and my editor felt that I needed to make the setting almost its own character so that readers would enjoy the familiar comfort of returning book-after-book.

That meant doing a lot of research into what it's like to work for a theme park, watching employee training videos, reading employee manuals, digging up funny anecdotes, and creating quirky minor characters who appear in each installment. I gained a binder full of authentic details and anecdotes from my research.

I also read books about setting, which refreshed my memory on how setting can convey conflict and the character's emotions. Incorporating these details has made the first book much stronger, and it will also make the series much stronger—not to mention easier to write— due to all my homework.

Karen Rose Smith: Caprice's Choco Chunks and Chips Cookies

This is a special recipe I developed to accompany my Caprice De Luca Home Staging Mystery Series. In addition to staging and redecorating clients' homes, Caprice De Luca loves everything retro. From a large Italian family, her relationships with her brother and sisters, parents and Nana Celia mean everything to her.

Caprice and her sisters learned to cook from their mom and Nana. Cooking together is bonding time, as are the monthly De Luca family dinners. In each Caprice De Luca Home Staging Mystery, solve the murder with Caprice, cook along with her, watch her find homes for the stray animals she protects, and be a part of the De Luca family.

Recipe yields approximately 30-36 cookies.

1/2 cup salted butter, softened
1/4 cup peanut butter
1 cup packed brown sugar
3/4 cup granulated sugar
2 large eggs
1/8 teaspoon cinnamon
3 teaspoons vanilla extract
1-1/2 teaspoons baking powder
1 teaspoon baking soda
3 cups flour
1-1/2 cups semi-sweet chocolate chips
6 ounces milk chocolate (I use two 3-ounce Dove bars broken into small pieces or chunks. These bars break or cut up easily.)

Preheat oven to 375 degrees F.

In a mixer, cream softened butter and peanut butter. Mix in brown sugar and granulated sugar until creamed. Add eggs and mix well. Add cinnamon and vanilla extract. Add baking powder and baking soda. Blend well. Add 2 cups of flour, 1/4 cup at a time with mixer on low speed, constantly scrapping bowl. Stir in the other cup of flour, 1/4 cup at a time, by hand until completely blended. Stir in chocolate chips and chunks.

Roll dough into 1-1/2" balls, place on cookie sheet 2 inches apart, and press down slightly with palm of hand. (I usually put 12 on one cookie sheet.)

Bake 11-12 minutes until golden brown and set. (The type of cookie sheet you use can affect the baking time. Darker cookie sheets bake faster.)

Remove from the oven and let the cookies sit a minute on a cool surface. Remove from pan. Allow to cool until the chocolate hardens. Unless you eat all of them gooey warm!

Karen Rose Smith is an award-winning and bestselling author who will see her eighty-sixth novel published in 2015. Although she has written romance novels for over twenty years, she has now branched out into mysteries and women's fiction. Writing for Kensington Books, Harlequin and indie publishing her Search For Love series, she still saves time for her four rescue cats, gardening, cooking, and photography. She has also developed many of her books into audiobooks. Read more about Karen and her books at www.karenrosesmith.com.

What's your recipe for a loving, lasting relationship?
Honesty, communication, and weekly date nights!

What's the best writing advice you ever received?
The best writing advice I ever received was from my dad who told me to "keep trying." After finishing thirteen manuscripts in six years I sold to two different publishers in a week. I've gone on to sell eighty-five more novels.

Made in the USA
Lexington, KY
28 September 2014